The
Spanish
Conquistadors

Don Nardo

LUCENT BOOKS
A part of Gale, Cengage Learning

Detroit • New York • San Francisco • New Haven, Conn • Waterville, Maine • London

LIBRARY OF CONGRESS CATALOGING-IN-PUBLICATION DATA

Nardo, Don, 1947–
    The Spanish conquistadors / by Don Nardo.
        p. cm. — (World history)
    Includes bibliographical references and index.
    ISBN 978-1-4205-0133-9 (hardcover)
    1. America—Discovery and exploration—Spanish—Juvenile literature. 2. Explorers—America—Biography—Juvenile literature. 3. Explorers—Spain—Biography—Juvenile literature. 4. Indians—First contact with Europeans—Juvenile literature. 5. Spaniards—America—History—Juvenile literature. I. Title.
    E123.N37 2009
    970.01'6—dc22

                                                          2008033730

Lucent Books
27500 Drake Rd.
Farmington Hills, MI 48331

ISBN-13: 978-1-4205-0133-9
ISBN-10: 1-4205-0133-X

Printed in the United States of America
1 2 3 4 5 6 7 13 12 11 10 09

Contents

Foreword

Each year, on the first day of school, nearly every history teacher faces the task of explaining why his or her students should study history. Many reasons have been given. One is that lessons exist in the past from which contemporary society can benefit and learn. Another is that exploration of the past allows us to see the origins of our customs, ideas, and institutions. Concepts such as democracy, ethnic conflict, or even things as trivial as fashion or mores, have historical roots.

Reasons such as these impress few students, however. If anything, these explanations seem remote and dull to young minds. Yet history is anything but dull. And therein lies what is perhaps the most compelling reason for studying history: History is filled with great stories. The classic themes of literature and drama—love and sacrifice, hatred and revenge, injustice and betrayal, adversity and overcoming adversity—fill the pages of history books, feeding the imagination as well as any of the great works of fiction do.

The story of the Children's Crusade, for example, is one of the most tragic in history. In 1212 Crusader fever hit Europe. A call went out from the pope that all good Christians should journey to Jerusalem to drive out the hated Muslims and return the city to Christian control. Heeding the call, thousands of children made the journey. Parents bravely allowed many children to go, and entire communities were inspired by the faith of these small Crusaders. Unfortunately, many boarded ships were captained by slave traders, who enthusiastically sold the children into slavery as soon as they arrived at their destination. Thousands died from disease, exposure, and starvation on the long march across Europe to the Mediterranean Sea. Others perished at sea.

Another story, from a modern and more familiar place, offers a soul-wrenching view of personal humiliation but also the ability to rise above it. Hatsuye Egami was one of 110,000 Japanese Americans sent to internment camps during World War II. "Since yesterday we Japanese have ceased to be human beings," he wrote in his diary. "We are numbers. We are no longer Egamis, but the number 23324. A tag with that number is on every trunk, suitcase and bag. Tags, also, on our breasts." Despite such dehumanizing treatment, most internees worked hard to control their bitterness. They created workable communities inside the camps and demonstrated again and again their loyalty as Americans.

These are but two of the many stories from history that can be found in the pages of the Lucent Books World History series. All World History titles rely on sound research and verifiable evidence, and all give students a clear sense of time, place, and chronology through maps and timelines as well as text.

All titles include a wide range of authoritative perspectives that demonstrate the complexity of historical interpretation and sharpen the reader's critical thinking skills. Formally documented quotations and annotated bibliographies enable students to locate and evaluate sources, often instantaneously via the Internet, and serve as valuable tools for further research and debate.

Finally, Lucent's World History titles present rousing good stories, featuring vivid primary source quotations drawn from unique, sometimes obscure sources such as diaries, public records, and contemporary chronicles. In this way, the voices of participants and witnesses as well as important biographers and historians bring the study of history to life. As we are caught up in the lives of others, we are reminded that we too are characters in the ongoing human saga, and we are better prepared for our own roles.

Important Dates

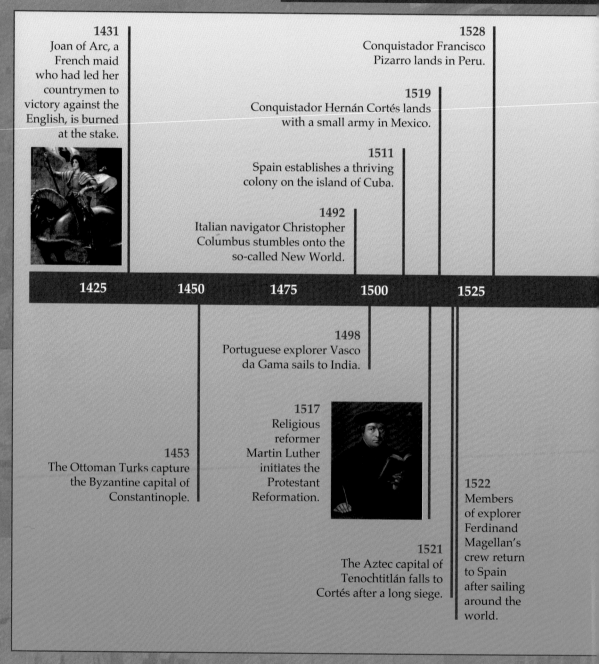

1431
Joan of Arc, a French maid who had led her countrymen to victory against the English, is burned at the stake.

1528
Conquistador Francisco Pizarro lands in Peru.

1519
Conquistador Hernán Cortés lands with a small army in Mexico.

1511
Spain establishes a thriving colony on the island of Cuba.

1492
Italian navigator Christopher Columbus stumbles onto the so-called New World.

1425	1450	1475	1500	1525

1498
Portuguese explorer Vasco da Gama sails to India.

1517
Religious reformer Martin Luther initiates the Protestant Reformation.

1453
The Ottoman Turks capture the Byzantine capital of Constantinople.

1522
Members of explorer Ferdinand Magellan's crew return to Spain after sailing around the world.

1521
The Aztec capital of Tenochtitlán falls to Cortés after a long siege.

of the Period

1533
Pizarro orders the execution of the Inca leader Atahuallpa.

1541
Gonzalo Pizarro sets out to find the legendary kingdom of El Dorado.

1547
Ivan the Terrible becomes czar of Russia, initiating a brutal reign.

1588
The English defeat the Spanish Armada, preventing an invasion of their homeland.

| 1540 | 1550 | 1560 | 1570 | 1580 |

1542
Conquistador Francisco de Orellana emerges into the Atlantic Ocean after a harrowing voyage down the Amazon River.

1589
The so-called "last conquistador" dies after apologizing for Spain's conquests of the Native Americans.

1572
In Peru the last Inca stronghold falls to the Spanish.

1536
English king Henry VIII beheads his wife, Anne Boleyn.

An Epic Conquest Reevaluated

The term *conquistador* comes from the Spanish word *conquistar*, meaning "to conquer," so a literal translation would be "conqueror." But for the past few centuries, the term has had a more specific meaning. It has referred to a group of Spanish explorers, soldiers, and adventurers who took part in their country's invasion and seizure of newly discovered lands in the Americas in the 1500s. These individuals may not have fully appreciated the far-reaching consequences of their actions. As it turned out, their conquests were no less than epic in scope. They constituted "one of the most cataclysmic events [violent upheavals] in history," as scholar Michael Wood aptly puts it. In only a couple of generations, these invasions "overthrew the last high civilizations which had arisen independently on earth. [Few] events, if any in history, match these for sheer drama, endurance, and the incredible distances covered. And the conquest is still within living history. Its effects are still with us, working themselves out now across the globe."[1]

The "New World" vs. the "Old World"

One of these global effects was to open up vast new territories for European settlement. But as Wood says, this was done at the expense of the Native Americans who already occupied what Europeans called the "New World." This term was meant to contrast the unknown lands of the Americas with the "Old World," comprised of Europe, Africa, and Asia. It is now plain that this was a highly biased way of looking at it. From the point of view of the Native Americans, or Indians (as explorer Christopher Columbus dubbed them), America was neither new nor unknown. It was their home and had been the home of countless generations of their ancestors.

Sadly for the native inhabitants of the New World, however, most Europeans had little or no concern for their views, beliefs, and sensibilities. Indeed, to the conquistadors the Indians were both uncivilized and heathens (non-Christians). Exactly who they were and how they had gotten to the Americas, no one could say for sure. What was more certain to the Spanish and other newcomers was that the natives were inferior. Their technology was primitive in comparison to that of the Europeans. Also, most of the natives had no cities; went naked, or nearly so, much of the time; and did not recognize Jesus Christ

An illustration from a Mexican Indian picture history depicts Spanish conquistadors and their Tlaxcalan Indian allies in battle against Tarascan warriors. European explorers looked upon the native peoples they encountered during their colonization of the "New World" as inferior and even subhuman, a point of view that allowed them to justify the brutality of their conquest.

and other aspects of the "one true faith" practiced across Europe.

Priests, scholars, and others in the Old World went so far as to debate whether the Native Americans were fully human and had souls. The renowned Spanish thinker and theologian Juan Ginés de Sepúlveda placed the Indians somewhere "between apes and men." This clearly made them inferior and seemed to justify imposing European rule and beliefs on them. According to Sepúlveda:

> The Spanish have a perfect right to rule these barbarians of the New World . . . who in prudence, skill, virtues, and humanity are as inferior to the Spanish as children to adults, or women to men. . . . Although some of them show a certain ingenuity for various works of artisanship [craftsmanship], this is no proof of human cleverness, for we can observe animals, birds, and spiders making certain structures which no human accomplishment can competently imitate. . . . Therefore, if you wish to [subdue] them . . . it will not be difficult for them to change their masters [and] accept the Christians, cultivators of human virtues and the true faith.[2]

The Debate at Valladolid

These were some of the arguments that Sepúlveda made at a then controversial debate that took place in 1550. Because it was held in the Spanish city of Valladolid, it became known as the "Valladolid debate." Various theologians, thinkers, and political figures gathered to discuss how the Native Americans should be treated. Most of those present agreed with Sepúlveda that the Indians were inferior. They were "natural slaves," as defined by the ancient Greek thinker Aristotle, and should be treated as such.

But a few of those at the conference disagreed. One, who emerged as Sepúlveda's chief opponent, was a Dominican friar named Bartolomé de Las Casas. He had moved to the Caribbean island of Hispaniola in 1502, only ten years after Columbus's fateful first voyage had introduced the New World to Europe. And he had personally witnessed the horrendous brutalities perpetrated on the natives by the Spanish. In his treatise, titled *A Brief Account of the Destruction of the Indies*, he calls the conquistadors' conquests and subsequent Spanish colonization cruel, unjust, and a form of extermination. He states:

> They treated them . . . not as beasts, [but] as the most abject dung and filth of the Earth; [and] the [natives] died without understanding the true Faith [i.e., Christianity] or Sacraments. And this also is as really true as [the fact] that the Spaniards never received any injury from the Indians, but that they [the natives] rather reverenced them [the Spanish] as persons descended from Heaven, until that they were compelled to take up arms, provoked [to do so] by repeated injuries, violent torments, and unjust butcheries.[3]

Las Casas argued that the American natives were fellow human beings. And as such, they should be educated to become Spanish subjects with the same rights as other Spaniards. To massacre some and enslave the rest, he warned, would prove disastrous in the end. Las Casas predicted that sooner or later the Spanish would suffer divine retribution. God would demolish the great empire Spain was building atop the mangled bodies and crushed souls of an unfairly oppressed people.

Needless to say, few Spaniards or other Europeans agreed with Las Casas. Kings and religious leaders eagerly justified the conquistadors' campaigns, saying that they were actually helping the natives by "civilizing" them. Thus, the colonization of the Americas proceeded at an unrelenting pace. And many tribes and peoples across North and South America lost their lands, had to convert to Christianity, and in some cases were eradicated.

Reevaluating the Conquistadors' Role

Today, nearly everyone agrees that these conquests were motivated by racism, religious intolerance, greed, and ignorance. But it should be recalled that this outlook emerged only recently. As late as the 1930s, many people still justified and romanticized the gory deeds of the conquistadors. They matter-of-factly accepted the view expressed in the 1840s by a leading American historian, who said the following about conquistador Hernán Cortés's subjugation of the Aztecs in Mexico: "If he destroyed the ancient capital of the Aztecs, it was to build up a more magnificent [European] capital on its ruins. If he desolated the land, [he introduced] there a more improved culture and a higher civilization. . . . The path of the conqueror is necessarily marked with blood."[4]

Indeed it was not until the twentieth century that the vast global empires of the Spanish and other Europeans were dismantled and numerous native peoples gained their independence. One by-product of this process has been a reevaluation of the conquistadors' role in history. Increasingly, they have been portrayed as naked aggressors who dealt with the Native Americans cruelly and unjustly. Perhaps somewhere Las Casas is smiling. Though it took a very long time, much of the world finally came around to his belief that all people deserve respect and decent treatment.

Chapter One

Rise of the Spanish Empire

The conquistadors, soldiers of fortune who explored and conquered vast sectors of North and South America, did not operate in a vacuum. They were the most daring and militant members of an army of Spanish explorers, settlers, and traders who exploited the newly found Americas in the 1500s. Spain had only recently emerged as a strong nation-state. And these adventurers swiftly acquired new Spanish-controlled territories around the globe, in less than a generation creating an empire that was then second to none. "In an amazingly brief period of time," historian William H. McNeill writes, the Spanish "proceeded to explore, conquer, and colonize the New World with extraordinary energy [and] utter ruthlessness."[5] By the end of the 1500s Spain had gained total or partial control of Cuba, Mexico, Florida, Panama, Venezuela, Peru, and several neighboring regions—encompassing millions of square miles in all. Thus, the story of the conquistadors is bound up in a larger narrative. In the course of its events, Spain emerged onto the world stage in what was then seen as a blaze of glory.

Emergence of a United Spain

Spain's tremendous success as both a new nation and an empire was due largely to the vision and efforts of two extraordinary rulers, Isabella I and Ferdinand II. Isabella (1451–1504) was queen of the Spanish kingdom of Castile. Ferdinand (1452–1516) was king of the neighboring kingdom of Aragon. When they were born, their kingdoms were among five separate ones—four Christian and one Muslim—that encompassed the Iberian peninsula. Westernmost, on the Atlantic coast, was Portugal. Castile occupied the peninsula's central region, while Aragon and tiny Navarre were arrayed in the north. The small Muslim kingdom of Granada lay in the far south.

Isabella and Ferdinand's unification of Castile, Aragon, Navarre, and Granada into a single, strong Spanish nation was the first of two major accomplishments that made the Spanish empire possible. Back in 1454, when Isabella was a three-year-old princess, her stepbrother, Enrique (Henry), became king of Castile. At the time, the idea of a unified Spain was controversial, and few

took it seriously. As she grew up, Isabella became one of those few. Politically astute beyond her years, as well as ambitious, she wisely saw that the Spanish kingdoms could not achieve greatness if they remained divided. And she dreamed of becoming queen of all Spaniards.

To that end, while still a teenager Isabella persuaded King Enrique to name

Spain in the 1500s

Spain's Inspirational Leader

Isabella and Ferdinand's unification of Spain was a long, difficult process fraught with obstacles and dangers. One of the biggest obstacles they overcame was an invasion of Castile in 1475 by some twenty thousand soldiers under Alfonso V, king of Portugal. When Isabella heard that some Spanish troops had retreated from the enemy, she made an impassioned speech to her soldiers, revealing herself to be a strong, inspirational leader. She said in part:

There must first be a battle in order to be a victory. [I] find myself in my palace, with angry heart and closed teeth and clenched fists. . . . Of my fury, being a woman, and of your patience, being men, I marvel. [The] ill-effect on your service on the kingdom, on foreign opinion and on the honor of our honors hurts. I bare my soul, because it is not within myself, suffering in spirit, that I can alleviate the pain, nor drive it out; for it is certain that the best rest for the afflicted is to vent their ills.

Quoted in Peggy K. Liss, *Isabel the Queen: Life and Times.* New York: Oxford University Press, 1992, p. 117.

her as heir to the Castilian throne. She also obtained his promise not to force her to marry against her wishes. Already, it seems, she had set her sights on marrying her distant cousin, Ferdinand, heir to the throne of Aragon. On the one hand, he was handsome, charming, and intelligent. But on the other hand, and more important, their wedding could lead to the union of their two realms, an important step in the creation of a greater Spain.

Isabella's plan unfolded as she had intended. She and Ferdinand married in 1469. Then, just five years later, Enrique died, leaving Isabella in charge of Castile. Immediately, she and Ferdinand began ruling their two kingdoms jointly, as if the two lands were one. Their motto became "Isabella is the same as Ferdinand," indi-cating that each had a share in ruling the other's land. They also set about healing old wounds caused by former disagreements and civil wars among the Spanish kingdoms. This created a new sense of peace and security that made them extremely popular. A historian of that era recorded how the two young rulers were "very celebrated" for "their wisdom and for having brought great tranquility and order into their realms that had formerly been most turbulent."[6]

Isabella and Ferdinand's unification efforts did not stop with their native kingdoms. They also undertook the then difficult and expensive task of conquering the Muslim stronghold of Granada. After years of persistent assaults, in January 1492 Granada fell. At that point, the only Spanish territory that remained outside of Isabella and Ferdinand's control was Navarre. (He finally brought it into the fold in 1512.) For all intents and purposes, Spain was now a viable nation that could compete with Portugal, France, England, and other major countries of the day.

Columbus's Accidental Discovery

Isabella and Ferdinand's other pivotal contribution to the establishment of Spain's empire was their sponsorship of the famous initial voyage of Christopher Columbus. An Italian, Columbus asked for ships with which to navigate the Atlantic Ocean. His main goal was to establish a quicker route to the "East Indies," the name Europeans then used to describe the little-known islands lying along Asia's eastern coast. (In those days, vessels had to sail around Africa to reach Asia, which took a long time.) He told the Spanish rulers that when he reached eastern Asia, or the "Far East," he would establish valuable trade routes. These would surely make Spain rich.

Of course, like other Europeans, Columbus did not realize that a vast land-mass—the Americas, along with another ocean, the Pacific—lay between

Queen Isabella and King Ferdinand, on horseback, accept the surrender of King Boalbdil, the Moorish king of Granada, in 1492, thus making the region part of the Spanish Empire.

Europe and the Far East. And his accidental discovery of the Americas in 1492 changed the situation considerably. The Spanish now found themselves with access to more than mere trade routes. Seemingly ripe for the taking were large, previously unknown territories that could provide Spain with a huge overseas empire.

One potential obstacle stood in the way of this opportunity. Namely, the Americas were already inhabited. However, Columbus quickly made it clear to his sponsors that this obstacle could easily be dealt with. The natives possessed technology and weapons far less advanced than those of the Europeans, he said. So the so-called Indians could be conquered and exploited with minimal effort. In a letter to Spanish officials, he explains:

All these people lack . . . every kind of iron. They are also without [advanced] weapons, which indeed are unknown; nor are they competent to use them. . . . When I sent two or three of my men to some of the villages, that they might speak with the natives, a compact troop of the Indians would march out, and as soon as

Christopher Columbus and members of his expedition to the New World are depicted showing various items to the natives they encountered upon landing in the Americas in 1492. Columbus assured Spanish officials that the natives could be easily conquered and would not pose a threat to colonization.

Columbus Communicates with the Natives

In 1493 Christopher Columbus wrote to Spain's King Ferdinand, saying how, after landing in the West Indies, he had managed to communicate with the natives and how at first they thought he and his men were heavenly beings:

As soon as I reached that sea, I seized by force several Indians on the first island, in order that they might learn from us, and in like manner tell us about those things in these lands of which they themselves had knowledge; and the plan succeeded, for in a short time we understood them and they us, sometimes by gestures and signs, sometimes by words; and it was a great advantage to us. They are coming with me now, yet always believing that I descended from heaven, although they have been living with us for a long time, and are living with us today. And these men were the first who announced it wherever we landed, continually proclaiming to the others in a loud voice, "Come, come, and you will see the celestial people."

Christopher Columbus, "The Columbus Letter: Translation," University of Southern Maine. www.usm.maine.edu/~maps/columbus/translation.html.

they saw our men approaching, they would quickly take flight . . . not because any hurt or injury had been inflicted on any one of them [but because] they are by nature fearful and timid.[7]

Columbus went on to say that with only fifty men he could subjugate all the Indians he had seen and force them to do whatever he wanted.

Motives for Empire

As Columbus did, Isabella, Ferdinand, and later Spanish leaders viewed the newly found lands and peoples across the sea strictly as commodities to be exploited. These leaders readily grasped the potential economic benefits for their country and sent out more explorers, along with soldiers and colonizers. Their overall motives have often been summarized in the familiar adage "God, glory, and gold." In this case, "God" meant the desire to convert the non-Christian natives to Christianity. "We have ordered some of our captains," says Isabella in a letter to her daughter, "to take with them some monks in order to indoctrinate and preach our holy Catholic faith."[8] "Glory" in the adage referred to the increased prestige Spain would enjoy as a result of building an empire.

However, to the Spanish the third motive in the adage, "gold," was much more important than the first two. Here, the term *gold* is shorthand for wealth, or riches, including gold, silver, and other precious metals; land; timber and other raw materials; and spices, fabrics, slaves, and other valuable commodities. Columbus himself concisely summed up the importance of the lure of wealth when he said, "With gold, one may do what one wishes in the world."[9]

It was plain that this philosophy could be expressed and exploited by a nation as well as an individual. And this was

Queen Isabella and King Ferdinand are depicted receiving a gracious Christopher Columbus in their court, accompanied by natives, fellow sailors, and the spoils of his expedition to the New World.

certainly the case with Spain as it entered its imperial age. The lust for riches was displayed most vividly and, regrettably, most brutally by Spain's chief empire builders, the conquistadors. A prominent member of Isabella's court, Gonzalo Fernández de Oviedo, who knew several of these men, later frankly described their base motives: "They are the sort of men who have no intention of converting the Indians or settling and remaining in this land. They come only to get some gold or wealth in whatever form they can obtain it. They subordinate honor, morality, and honesty to this end and apply themselves to any fraud or homicide and commit innumerable crimes."[10] This eagerness, indeed almost desperation, to find gold and become rich overnight is telling in another way. It explains why the conquistadors and other Spaniards were so quick to believe any and all rumors about buried treasures and cities having streets paved with gold hidden in unexplored regions of the Americas.

Another important motivating factor in Spain's rapid creation of an empire was the strong desire to outdo the Portuguese. In addition to being Spain's neighbor on the Iberian peninsula, Portugal was also its traditional rival and quite often its enemy. Even while Isabella and Ferdinand were laboring to unite Spain, the Portuguese were beginning to create their own overseas empire. They began settling the Madeira Islands, in the eastern Atlantic, in the 1420s and the Azores, also in the Atlantic, in the 1440s. The Portuguese also established valuable colonies in western Africa and in 1488

rounded that continent's southern tip, opening up trade routes to the Far East.

Hoping to surpass Portugal, the Spanish stepped up their efforts in the race for empire. Castile took complete control of another Atlantic island group—the Canaries—in 1496. The Spanish also began making inroads into Africa the following year. But these gains paled in comparison to those made possible by explorers in the New World.

Hispaniola and Beyond

Indeed, in 1493, barely a year after Columbus had first landed on the large Caribbean island of Hispaniola (now home to Haiti and the Dominican Republic), large numbers of Spanish settlers arrived there. They established a capital, Santo Domingo (the oldest permanent European settlement in the Americas). They also began to develop the island's potential as a home base for exploring and seizing nearby islands.

The most striking and controversial acts committed by the Spanish in Hispaniola were those connected with their exploitation and mistreatment of the natives. In this regard, they established a precedent and a pattern that would be repeated time and again in other parts of the Americas. Between 1493 and 1515 Hispaniola's new masters worked to death or outright murdered 80 percent of Hispaniola's original 250,000 residents. According to Las Casas, who lived on the island in the early 1500s:

They [the Spanish soldiers] laid wagers among themselves, [as to] who should with a sword at one blow cut, or divide, a man in two; or which of them should . . . behead a man with the greatest dexterity [or] sheath his sword in the bowels of a man [the] quickest. . . . They snatched young babes from the mothers' breasts, and then dashed out the brains of those innocents against the rocks; others they cast into rivers, scoffing and jeering them. . . . [The Spanish officers also] ordered gridirons [metal barbecues] to be placed and supported with wooden forks, and putting a small fire under them, [they roasted] these miserable wretches by degrees, and with loud shrieks [the poor souls] at last expired [died]. I once saw four or five of their most powerful lords laid on these gridirons, and thereon roasted. . . . [Their cries were] offensive to the Captain, [who] commanded them to be strangled. . . . I was an eye-witness of these and an innumerable number of other cruelties [perpetrated by the Spanish on the island].[11]

Spanish captors violently subdue slaves after an attempted escape. In just over two decades following Columbus's arrival, eighty percent of the native population of Hispaniola was exterminated at the hands of the Europeans.

Massacre of the Cuban Indians

Spaniard Bartolomé de Las Casas witnessed firsthand the colonization of several islands in the West Indies by the Spanish. And he recorded for posterity the brutal treatment of the natives. In this excerpt from his narrative, he describes the forced labor and murders perpetrated by Spanish settlers in Cuba in the early 1500s.

A certain [Spanish landowner] here [tried] to exercise a kind of royal power. [He] happened to have three hundred Indians fall [under his control], of which in three months, through excessive labor, one hundred and sixty were destroyed. [Not long afterward] there remained but a tenth part alive, namely thirty [Indians], but [eventually] they all perished. . . . In three or four months time, I being there present, six thousand [or more] children were murdered, because they had lost their parents, who [had] labored in the mines, [and] I was a witness of many other stupendous villainies [crimes]. But afterward they [the Spanish] consulted how to persecute those [Indians] that lay hid[den] in the mountains, who were miserably massacred, and consequently this isle made desolate.

Bartolomé de Las Casas, *A Brief Account of the Destruction of the Indies*, Project Gutenberg, 2007. www. gutenberg.org/files/20321/20321-8.txt.

Only five hundred of Hispaniola's Indians were left by 1550. And by 1650 all had been exterminated.

Another atrocity perpetrated early on in Spain's new American colonies involved efforts to Christianize the natives. Spanish leaders, including most of the conquistadors, partly justified their seizure of Indian lands by claiming they were saving their souls. Yet though some Indians were converted, this was mostly fiction. Large numbers of natives were brutalized and killed without any exposure to Christian ideas. Moreover, those who did learn Christian ways also had to swear allegiance to the Spanish king. Las Casas was one of a small handful of Spanish who saw how unjust and un-Christian these practices were. It was "as if," he writes,

the Son of God, who suffered death for the redemption of all mankind, had enacted a law, demanding that [non-Christians] living peaceably and quietly in their [native] country, should be [forced], upon pain of confiscation of all their [property], lands, liberty, wives, [and] children . . . to confess and acknowledge the true God, and subject themselves to a king whom they never saw or heard mentioned before, and whose messengers behaved [with] such inhumanity and cruelty.[12]

The natives of Hispaniola were not the only Indians to suffer from the onslaught of Spanish settlers, traders, and soldiers. Other Caribbean islands were swiftly colonized. One of the largest and most productive of these was Cuba, where Spaniards planted their first colony in 1511. (Havana, long the island's biggest city, was founded in 1515.) In their zeal to grow and export valuable cash crops, especially sugar, coffee, and tobacco, the Spanish enslaved tens of thousands of natives and subjected them to forced labor. Those who resisted too much were slaughtered.

Cuba and other nearby islands proved particularly important in the story of the conquistadors. These islands were located quite close to the shores of the North American mainland, including what is now Mexico. Adventurers, including Francisco Fernández de Córdoba, Juan de Grijalba, and the famous Hernán Cortés, heard stories and rumors about Mexico, which was then unexplored by Europeans. They believed it could be a source of gold, slaves, and other riches, a virgin land ready to be exploited. First contact with Mexico occurred in 1517 under Córdoba. And Cortés initiated the first major Spanish conquest of the mainland just two years later. The conquistadors were about to put the Spanish empire, along with themselves, squarely on the map of history.

Chapter Two

Cortés's Mexican Adventure

The first major conquest carried out by a Spanish conquistador was the subjugation of the Aztecs in Mexico by Cortés. It is important to emphasize that the term *Aztec* is a misnomer. The native people that Cortés defeated called themselves the Tenochcas, or Mexicas, and in fact, Cortés and other Spaniards of his day called them Mexicas. The term *Aztec* was artificially coined by scholars much later, in the nineteenth century. It is used in this and other modern books mainly because of its subsequent wide acceptance and familiarity.

The Aztecs appear to have migrated from what is now northern Mexico into the Valley of Mexico (south-central Mexico) in the 1200s A.D. They established their capital, Tenochtitlán, on an island in Lake Texcoco in about 1325. And in the following century they conquered most of the surrounding native peoples. Thus, when Cortés and his men arrived in Mexico in 1519, they found a large

Aztec empire stretching from the Gulf of Mexico in the east to the Pacific Ocean in the west.

Cortés was not the first Spaniard to see this region of North America. In 1517 conquistador Francisco Fernández de Córdoba sailed with four ships and 110 men from Cuba to the coast of the Yucatán peninsula (in southeastern Mexico). There he met with some local Mayan Indians. But soon the Spaniards came under attack, took heavy losses, and headed back to Cuba. In April of the following year, another conquistador, Juan de Grijalba, also landed in the Yucatán and suffered losses. Before leaving, however, he communicated with some of the natives. They told him about a great city built on a lake far inland. It was the center of a vast empire, they said, whose rulers controlled the Mayans of the Yucatán and many other peoples. Both Córdoba and Grijalba had reason to believe that this empire and its leaders were rich in

A map depicts the Aztec capital of Tenochtitlán, which was established around 1325, surrounded by the waters of Lake Texcoco.

gold. That was enough to whet the appetite of other Spaniards, including Cortés, who soon mounted his own expedition to Mexico.

Genesis of Cortés's Expedition

Hernán Cortés (sometimes spelled Hernando Cortéz), whom history came to call the "conqueror of Mexico," was born in 1484 in the Castilian town of Medellín. Numerous men from the many fortified towns surrounding Medellín fought against the Muslims in Granada and/or as mercenaries in wars in Italy. It is not surprising, therefore, that many conquistadors came from this region of Castile.

Not much is known about Cortés's early life and education. As a young man he wandered throughout Spain, apparently seeking adventure. To this end, in 1506, at age twenty-two, he journeyed to the East Indies and settled in Hispaniola. He quickly gained a reputation as a gambler and womanizer. Three years later, Cortés moved to Cuba, where, by raising cattle and exploiting Indian slaves, he became one of the richest men on the island. Yet this was not enough to satisfy him. It seems that he believed he was destined for everlasting fame and once told some friends that he would "either die to the sound of trumpets or die on the scaffold."[13]

Perhaps sensing that money and fame might come from exploiting the then still mysterious Mexican mainland, Cortés helped to raise funds for Juan de Grijalba's expedition. Its failure was no doubt a considerable disappointment. However, a greater opportunity soon materialized. In 1518 Cuba's Spanish governor, Diego Velásquez, approached Cortés about a new and larger Mexican expedition. Velásquez offered to provide a few ships and some money if Cortés could raise the rest of the money and men needed. The governor also named Cortés the venture's leader. According to one of Cortés's close associates, Francisco de Aguilar, the newly appointed "captain-general" wasted no time: "Cortés devoted himself to the undertaking with such ability and industriousness, as the astute man that he was, that in a few days he had obtained funds borrowed from among his friends, and enlisted another two hundred men, and secured a large supply of provisions."[14]

But when Velásquez heard of the large amount of money and men Cortés was raising, he had second thoughts. Perhaps the governor reasoned that Cortés was too ambitious and might steal most of the glory and riches from Velásquez himself. According to Aguilar, "regretting his decision," Velásquez "tried to take the armada [fleet] away from Cortés, and went to the port with some men to carry this out. But the shrewd Hernán Cortés, taking advantage of the lateness of the day, and the good weather, raised anchor, hoisted sail, and left."[15]

Thus, when Cortés departed Cuba, he did so in defiance of the local Spanish government. The only way he could avoid eventual arrest and execution would be to achieve huge success in the undertaking and bring Spain great riches and prestige. It was an enormous gamble, even for an experienced gambler like himself. But he was willing to take the risk. It may be that some of

Spanish explorer Hernán Cortés spent more than a decade as a settler in Hispaniola and Cuba before launching his expedition to Mexico.

Cortés and members of his expedition bid farewell to Diego Velásquez, Cuba's Spanish governor, as they set sail for Mexico.

his confidence was based on the large number of people, weapons, and supplies he had collected. They included eleven ships; 530 Europeans, including many experienced soldiers; several hundred Cuban Indians and Africans, some slave and some free; a doctor and some carpenters; a number of crossbows and handheld guns (primitive front-loaders called arquebuses); nearly twenty cannons; sixteen horses; and many large dogs trained for warfare.

Initial Contacts in Mexico

With this array of people and equipment, Cortés crossed to the Yucatán coast in late February 1519. From the ships he and his followers could see Mayan pyramids rising from the nearby forests. Some initial contact was made with local Mayans, and through sign language Cortés learned that a Spaniard was living among the natives in a nearby town. That man soon arrived on the beach. His name was Geronimo de Aguilar, and he explained that he had been shipwrecked eight years before. This was a stroke of luck for Cortés because he now had someone who could translate the Mayan language into Spanish.

The expedition next sailed northward around the Yucatán to the mouth of the Tabasco River. When the Spaniards went ashore, some local natives gave them a cool reception and told them to

A native woman who was originally a servant to the Spaniards, Malinche, right, used her knowledge of languages to serve as a translator for the expedition and eventually became Cortés's constant companion.

go away. Unwilling to be intimidated, Cortés refused, after which a large group of Indians appeared. According to an account later written by one of Cortés's men, these natives were

armed with bows, arrows, lances, and bucklers [small shields], and shouting to us to leave the land, but if we wanted war, to begin at once. . . . [Cortés] ordered us to fire the guns and attack. A few of us were wounded when the shots were fired and as our men were landing, but at last the speed of our attack . . . drove them out of the village, [which] we took [and] occupied.[16]

Though small-scale and brief, this battle was pivotal for Cortés. It showed him the "shocking impact" of artillery on "people who had never seen guns," in Michael Wood's words. "The Spanish weaponry meant that, even outnumbered ten to one, they could still expect victory at little cost to themselves."[17]

Indeed, awed by Spanish firepower the defeated locals became submissive and supplied the newcomers with gifts, food, and servants. Among the latter was a woman named Malinche. According to Francisco de Aguilar, "She knew the Mexican tongue [Nahuatl, the language spoken by the Aztecs] and understood the [Mayan] language [as well], and this news pleased everyone in the company."[18] Fortune had smiled on Cortés again. He had heard that the local coastal towns were part of a great empire ruled by the Aztecs. And he

From Spaniard to Mayan Warrior

When Cortés landed in Mexico, he encountered Geronimo de Aguilar, a Spaniard who had been shipwrecked on the Yucatán coast eight years before and lived among the local Mayans. Another Spanish conquistador who survived that shipwreck was Gonzalo Guerrero. At first, he was enslaved by the natives. But he eventually earned his freedom and became a widely respected Mayan warrior. He also married a rich Mayan woman and raised what modern scholars believe were the first mestizo (mixed-race) children in Central America.

now had a translator who would prove valuable when he confronted that people's messengers and leaders. In fact, Malinche became more than a mere translator. Cortés made her his mistress and personal adviser, and thereafter the two always appeared in public together.

The Massacre at Cholula

From the Tabasco River Cortés sailed farther northwestward to a small island the Spanish called the Isle of Sacrifices. There they met some local Indians, the Totonacs, who gave them a friendly welcome. Not long afterward, some messengers sent by the great leader of the Aztecs arrived. They said that he, Motecuhzoma (now more often called Montezuma), had heard about the newcomers' arrival and their battle with the Mayans in the Yucatán. The messengers had been ordered to open diplomatic negotiations with Cortés and to offer him and his men food and shelter.

The Spaniards accepted these things and also made a point of demonstrat-ing their military might. They fired off their cannons, which caused the Aztec ambassadors to fall to the ground in fear. It was now clearer than ever to Cortés that his advantages—guns, steel, and horses—were major ones. If used wisely, they might make it possible for his small army to conquer the natives without reinforcements from the Spanish colonies.

To further increase his chances of success, Cortés shrewdly considered enlisting the aid of the Aztecs' local enemies. From the coastal Indians he learned that the Aztecs used force to keep several neighboring subject peoples in line and as a result were hated by these peoples. Cortés also heard about the Tlaxcalans. Traditional enemies of the Aztecs, they lived to the east of the Aztec capital Tenochtitlán and had never come under the Aztecs' control.

For these reasons, Cortés decided that his wisest course of action was to team up with the Tlaxcalans and march on Tenochtitlán. It was a daring plan, especially considering that he had not discussed it with Spanish authorities. And he wanted to make sure that none of his own men tried to return to Cuba and tell governor Velásquez what he was up to. So he ordered the sinking of his own ships before marching westward toward the Tlaxcalan capital.

To his dismay, Cortés found that the alliance with the Tlaxcalans was not easy to forge. They resisted at first. But after a few weeks they welcomed the opportunity to humble their longtime enemies, the Aztecs. Beforehand, however, the Tlax-calans wanted the Spanish to help them fight a people they hated even more than the Aztecs—the Cholulans, whose city of Cholula lay only thirty miles southwest of Tlaxcala. Obligingly, Cortés agreed. And soon his men were marching into Cholula's wide central square, in which an imposing pyramid rose.

The Spaniards later justified the massacre that followed by claiming that the leading Cholulans were plotting to kill them. Whether or not this was true, the Spaniards and their Indian allies attacked and slew several thousand

Cortés's troops are depicted in the midst of battle after invading Cholula at the request of the Tlaxcalans, who had allied themselves with the Spaniards in their quest to defeat the Aztecs. The attack left several thousand Indians dead.

Spanish War Dogs

When the conquistadors went to Mexico, they brought with them many large dogs, mostly mastiffs and wolfhounds, trained in both hunting and warfare. On command, these canines attacked, mauled, and in some cases killed unruly natives. A surviving Aztec account describes the Spanish dogs:

Their dogs are enormous, with flat ears and long, dangling tongues. The color of their eyes is a burning yellow, and their eyes flash fire and shoot off sparks. Their bellies are hollow, their flanks long and narrow. They are tireless and very powerful. They bound here and there, panting, with their tongues hanging out. And they are spotted like an ocelot.

Quoted in Miguel Leon-Portilla, ed., *The Broken Spears: The Aztec Account of the Conquest of Mexico.* Boston: Beacon, 1992, p. 31.

Cholulans. "They defended themselves the best they could," one of Cortés's captains, Andres de Tapia, later recalled. "But since they were walled inside the courtyards with the entrances guarded, most of them died anyway. This done, the Spaniards and Indians in our company went out in squads to different parts of the city, killing warriors and burning houses."[19]

An Ancient God's Return?

After the slaughter was over, Cortés, his men, and his native allies moved on toward Tenochtitlán. Soon, more ambassadors from Montezuma appeared. This time they offered the Spaniards gold necklaces, perhaps hoping they would be satisfied and go away. A surviving native account records the reactions of Cortés's officers: "When they were given these presents, the Spaniards burst into smiles. Their eyes shone with pleasure [and] they picked up the gold and fingered it like monkeys. . . . The truth is that they longed and lusted for gold. Their bodies swelled with greed [and] they hungered like pigs for that gold."[20]

The Spaniards' reaction to the gold must have worried the Aztec messengers. Certainly their leader back in Tenochtitlán was anxious about the approaching army of Europeans and Tlaxcalans. For weeks Montezuma had been meeting with his chief advisers, trying to decide who or what these bearded, steel-armored newcomers were. Some of the emperor's advisers argued that the Spaniards were simply ordinary men who had come to make war. But others thought they might be gods previously unknown to the Aztecs.

The most compelling theory was that Cortés might be Quetzalcoatl, a legendary figure from Mexico's past. Supposedly, he was a light-skinned, bearded sky god who had long ruled in the Valley of Mexico. Eventually he had departed eastward over the sea, saying that he would return someday. The fact that Cortés was light-skinned, bearded, and had come by sea from the east seemed to partially confirm the theory. Even more convincing to Montezuma was that the date that Aztec astrologers had predicted for Quetzalcoatl's return was 1519, the very year that Cortés had arrived in Mexico. "He has appeared!" Montezuma reportedly said in reference to Quetzalcoatl. "He has come back! He will come here, to the place of his throne . . . for that is what he promised when he departed!"[21]

Cortés and Montezuma Meet

Montezuma was therefore optimistic when Cortés's expedition arrived at the southern shore of Lake Texcoco in early November 1519. The Spaniards were amazed by their first sight of Tenochtitlán, which rested on an island connected to the shore by long, sturdy stone causeways. According to the account of one of Cortés's men:

The circumference of this city is from two and a half to three leagues. [A Spanish league then equaled about 2.6 miles (4.2km), so the city was almost 8 miles (13km) in circumference.] Most of the persons who have seen it judge it to have sixty thousand inhabitants or more. [The city] has many beautiful and wide streets [and] very beautiful squares [and] many beautiful houses belonging to the [Aztec] lords. They were so large and had so many rooms . . . that they were a sight to behold.[22]

The Aztecs offered no resistance as Cortés and his followers marched along a five-mile-long (8km) causeway and into the city. After a group of Aztecs performed a traditional ceremony of greeting, Montezuma appeared, decked

Montezuma, leader of the Aztecs, submits to Cortés his agreement to become a subject of the Spanish king, following his arrest by the Spanish invaders in November 1519.

A Deliberate Act of Terror?

Cortés claimed that the slaughter at Cholula occurred because the Cholulans were plotting to kill the Spaniards. However, some evidence suggests that there was no such plot. The Spanish monk Bartolomé de Las Casas later called the massacre a deliberate act of terror by Cortés designed to instill fear and awe in all Indians in the region. The Cholulans themselves agreed that the victims were blameless and said that the Tlaxcalans had urged the Spanish to kill their longtime enemies, the Cholulans. According to a surviving native account:

The sudden slaughter began. Knife strokes, and sword strokes, and death. The people of Cholula had not foreseen it, had not suspected it. They faced the Spaniards without weapons, without their swords or their shields. The cause of the slaughter was treachery. They died blindly, without knowing why, because of the lies of the Tlaxcalans.

Quoted in Miguel Leon-Portilla, ed., *The Broken Spears: The Aztec Account of the Conquest of Mexico.* Boston: Beacon, 1992, pp. 40–41.

out in his finest clothes and jewelry. The emperor briefly welcomed Cortés. In Francisco de Aguilar's words, he "placed necklaces of gold and precious stones about Cortés, and Cortés placed a string of painted beads about Montezuma's neck. With all courtesy, Montezuma bade him welcome, saying this was the captain's [Cortés's] home, and Cortés thanked him for such a kind reception."[23]

Longer, more formal speeches by the two leaders took place a while later in Montezuma's throne room. The exact words of these addresses are somewhat uncertain. But both the Spanish and native accounts agree that the leaders' tone was friendly.

This pleasantness and civility did not last long, however. Cortés had managed, without fighting and loss of men, to penetrate the capital of a vast and apparently wealthy kingdom. He did not want to take the chance of waiting too long to take advantage of such good fortune. After all, he reasoned, the longer he and his men remained guests in the city, the more likely the Aztecs would be to recognize that the strangers were ordinary humans, not gods. Therefore, on November 16, a little more than a week after arriving in Tenochtitlán, Cortés suddenly arrested Montezuma. The Spaniard told his hostage to go on governing his people but that he must do so according to Cortés's orders.

Montezuma was appalled at what was happening. He now realized that the newcomers were indeed only men and that he had been duped. But for the moment, he felt he had no other choice but to do as Cortés ordered. At some point, according to the Spanish accounts, the Aztec emperor agreed to become a subject of the Spanish king. However, modern scholars think it is likely that Montezuma did not fully understand what he was agreeing to.

An Audacious Gamble

For a few months Cortés continued to keep Montezuma hostage and to demand that he give the Spaniards gold and other valuables. Then, in April 1520 the situation altered dramatically when word came that more Spanish soldiers had landed on the Mexican coast. Governor Velásquez had sent an expedition led by Spanish nobleman Pánfilo de Narváez to arrest Cortés.

Realizing that his chances for riches and power were now in jeopardy, Cortés acted quickly. He left 120 of his men to maintain his hold on Tenochtitlán. Then he gathered the remainder of his army and raced for the coast, bent on stopping Narváez. It was another huge risk. Cortés was betting that, even after he had attacked and fought his own countrymen, the vast lands and riches he would acquire by conquest would persuade the king to forgive him. Only time would tell if this audacious gamble would pay off.

Chapter Three

The Conquest of Mexico

By April 1520 Hernán Cortés's Mexican expedition had achieved considerable military and political success. With very few losses it had marched hundreds of miles through densely populated native territory, enlisted thousands of Indian allies, entered the capital of the Aztec empire, and taken the Aztec emperor and his leading nobles captive. But suddenly, Cortés was in danger of suffering a complete reversal of fortune. A small army of more than eight hundred Spaniards had landed on the Mexican coast. Its commander, conquistador Pánfilo de Narváez, had orders to arrest Cortés for defying the authority of Cuba's governor.

Cortés realized that if he surrendered, his expedition would be over, and his place in history would be taken—in his view *stolen*—by others. So he decided to fight. He led a contingent of more than two hundred men eastward to the coast. And on a rainy night in May they launched a surprise attack on Narváez's camp. A letter Cortés later wrote to the Spanish king describes the raid and the capture of Narváez and his officers:

> When I [and my men] reached Narvaez's camp, all his men were armed and mounted and well prepared, [but] we came with such stealth that when they observed us and sounded the alarm, I was already inside the courtyard of the camp. . . . We reached the place where Narvaez slept, and he and some fifty men fought [against us, but finally] he surrendered. . . . With the loss of only two men, [in only] one hour all those whom we wished to capture were taken, together with [their weapons]. They promised to abide by Your Majesty's justice.[24]

In the scuffle Narváez lost an eye but survived. And Cortés promptly took charge of Narváez's soldiers. After hearing of Cortés's accomplishments and the riches he was beginning to exploit, they were glad to join his expedition. Once more he had beaten the odds and won a high-risk gamble. In the months that followed he would continue to act boldly, using whatever means he deemed necessary to achieve his goals. These were to bend the Aztecs and other natives to his will and to turn their lands into a Spanish colony.

The Toxcatl Massacre

To fulfill such ambitious goals Cortés needed officers he could trust to manage his affairs when he was away. His second in command, conquistador

An injured Pánfilo de Narváez, commander of a brigade sent to Mexico with orders to capture Cortés for his defiance of Cuba's governor, submits to defeat after a surprise attack by Cortés's men.

Pedro de Alvarado, was a prominent example. Shortly before hurrying off to fight Narváez, Cortés left Alvarado in charge of the Spanish forces occupying Tenochtitlán.

Cortés probably hoped that while he was gone, life in the chief Aztec city would be uneventful. But this did not happen. During these weeks Alvarado committed a number of violent acts against the natives, including burning some of them alive. He also ordered his men to launch a sneak attack on thousands of unarmed dancers and singers who were taking part in the annual Festival of Toxcatl.

This religious celebration honored Tezcatlipoca, the Aztec god of the night sky, war, beauty, and kingship. Each spring a young man (usually a war captive) was chosen to impersonate the god for a year. He was given fine clothes, good food,

With Cortés away to confront Narváez, his second in command, Pedro de Alvarado, and his men launched a brutal attack against unarmed natives celebrating the Festival of Toxcatl, horrifying the Aztecs and provoking their loss of faith in Montezuma's leadership.

Repulsed by Human Sacrifice

One Aztec tradition that repulsed the Spanish conquistadors was human sacrifice. On the one hand, the Aztecs did this in hope of appeasing their gods. On the other, it was part of an approach to warfare quite different from the one Europeans were accustomed to. The latter routinely killed their enemies in battle. When possible, the Aztecs preferred to kill their enemies after the battle was over, by sacrificing them. A surviving native account records some of the Spanish reactions to human sacrifice:

The envoys [sent to Cortés by Montezuma] sacrificed [some] captives in the presence of the strangers [Spanish], but when the white men saw this done, they were filled with disgust and loathing. They spat on the ground, or wiped away their tears, or closed their eyes and shook their heads in abhorrence [disgust]. They refused to eat the food that was sprinkled with blood.

Quoted in Miguel Leon-Portilla, ed., *The Broken Spears: The Aztec Account of the Conquest of Mexico*. Boston: Beacon, 1992, p. 33.

A native illustration depicts the Aztec ritual of sacrifice, in which captives are brought to an altar upon which a priest cuts their beating hearts from their chest. This was the fate of the Spaniards left behind when Cortés retreated from Tenochtitlán.

wives, and treated with great respect. The following spring, during the festival, priests sacrificed him to the god by removing his heart and placing his skull with those of victims who had been sacrificed in previous years. It was thought that this bloody rite, along with singing, dancing, and sacrifices of food and flowers, would appease Tezcatlipoca.

The massacre took place at the height of the festival in one of the city's main squares. According to one account, the Spaniards

posted guards so that no one could escape, and then rushed into the [courtyard] to slaughter the celebrants. [The Spaniards] ran in among the dancers, forcing their way to the place where the drums were played. They attacked the [drummer] and cut off his arms.

Then they cut off his head and it rolled across the floor. They attacked all the celebrants, stabbing them, spearing them, striking them with their swords. They attacked some of them from behind and these fell instantly to the ground with their entrails [insides] hanging out. Others they beheaded [or] split their heads to pieces [or] slashed others in the abdomen. [Their blood] flowed like water and gathered into pools.[25]

The reasons for this bloodbath are unclear. Some scholars suggest that Alvarado had evidence that the Aztec nobles were plotting to launch a rebellion while his commander was away. And he launched a preemptive strike to discourage such an uprising.

Whatever Alvarado's motivations may have been, his actions filled the Aztecs with confusion, horror, and revulsion. As Michael Wood points out, massacres of unarmed people were beyond their experience:

The Mexicans [Aztecs], for all their "fierce and unnatural cruelty," as the Spanish describe it . . . had very precise rules about the conduct of warfare, and very precise rules about violence to the human body. As their sacrificial ceremonies show, their cruelties were strictly controlled [and] ritualized. The idea of this kind of pre-emptive strike . . . was incredible to them. [For] them, it was the Spanish who exhibited "unnatural cruelty."[26]

"Have You Not Seen Hell?"

Spurred to action by the mass murder in the courtyard, Aztec warriors from other parts of the city gathered and retaliated against Alvarado's men. "The Aztecs attacked with javelins and arrows," a native account says. "They hurled their javelins with all their strength and the cloud of missiles spread out over the Spaniards like a yellow cloak. The Spaniards immediately took refuge in the palace."[27]

Thus, when Cortés returned a few days later he observed much hostility among the natives. And soon he and his troops were under siege in Montezuma's palace. "All the Indians in the city were preparing for war," in Cortés words, and they dismantled "all the bridges," hoping to keep the Spaniards from escaping. Some bloody skirmishes took place, some of which Cortés described: "I went out to attack the Indians in two or three places, and they fought very fiercely with us. [They] wounded me and many of the other Spaniards. We killed few of them, for they were sheltered from us on the other side of the bridges and threw stones on us from the roofs and terraces."[28]

The situation was so tense that Cortés felt he needed Montezuma's aid. He ordered the emperor to speak to his people from the palace roof and persuade them to disperse. By this time, however, the Aztecs no longer had any confidence in or respect for Montezuma. Seeing him as either a traitor or a pawn of the enemy, they hurled rocks at him, forcing him back into the palace. Some

Surrounded by his captors, Montezuma pleads in vain with enraged Aztec soldiers, provoked by the Toxcatl massacre, to end their attack against the Spaniards.

accounts say he was wounded in the incident. But if so, the extent of his injuries is unknown.

Unfortunately, this episode also sealed Montezuma's fate. Because he no longer had any influence over his people, he was of no further use to Cortés. The latter cold-heartedly ordered the execution of the emperor and all the Aztec nobles who were then in Spanish custody in the palace. The native leaders were strangled to death and their bodies were tossed from the rooftop into the courtyard below. Francisco de Aguilar later penned this vivid description of a group of native women coming to claim the bodies:

> After night fell, about ten o'clock, a terrifying mob of women appeared carrying torches. . . . They came for their husbands and relatives who lay dead in the [courtyard]. And they came for Montezuma, too.

And as the women recognized their men . . . they threw themselves upon them with great sorrow and grief, and raised such a wailing and crying that it filled one with fear. I was on guard duty then, and I said to my companion, "Have you not seen hell? For if you have not seen it, you may witness it from here." In truth, in all the war and in all the terrors I went through, I was never so afraid as when I heard that awful lamentation [expression of grief].[29]

The Night of Sorrows

This time Cortés had badly miscalculated. He had assumed that Montezuma's people, having turned on him, would not care if he and his main followers were executed. But the chief Spaniard was wrong. The Indians viewed the murders as the latest in a series of outrages committed against them and their nation by the outsiders. Cortés and his men now realized that a full-scale attack by tens of thousands of Aztecs was likely, if not certain. And even if the natives failed to break in, they could easily wear down and defeat the trapped men by depriving them of food and fresh water.

Clearly, the Spaniards had to find some way of escaping the city. They decided to sneak away in the middle of the night on July 1, 1519. Cortés chose the shortest of the several causeways leading to the lakeshore, and because the Aztecs had removed the bridges, he had his men construct a portable bridge out of roofing timbers. In addition to the more than twelve hundred Spaniards were at least a couple thousand Tlaxcalan allies. These Indians helped drag the cannons and carry tons of gold and other loot accumulated in the preceding few months. Hoping to remain undetected, Cortés told his men to wrap their horses' hooves with cloth and to communicate in whispers.

Some of the city's residents noticed what was happening, however, and raised an alarm. As drums sounded ominously from the top of one of the pyramids, thousands of Aztec warriors swiftly organized and went into action. Some swept onto the causeway, while others jumped into boats and assaulted its sides. As the killing began, many of the Spaniards and their Tlaxcalan allies panicked, and the crowded causeway became a hellish scene of chaos, screams of fear, and death. According to a surviving eyewitness account:

> The boats converged on the Spaniards [and] the warriors loosed a storm of arrows at the fleeing army. [When] the Spaniards reached the Canal of the Toltecs . . . they hurled themselves headlong into the water, as if they were leaping from a cliff [and] the canal was soon choked with the bodies of men and horses. They filled the gap in the causeway with their own drowned bodies. Those who followed crossed to the other side by walking on the corpses.[30]

This fateful event later came to be called the Noche Triste, or "Night of Sor-

The Battle on the Causeway

Conquistador Francisco de Aguilar later penned this description of the battle on the causeway during the Night of Sorrows:

They [the Aztec warriors] all ran out with their weapons to cut us off, following us with great fury, shooting arrows, spears, and stones, and wounding us with their swords. Here many Spaniards fell, some dead and some wounded, and others without any injury who fainted away from fright. And since all of us were fleeing, there was not a man who would lift a hand to help his companion, or even his own father. . . . As we were fleeing, it was heartbreaking to see our companions dying, and to see how the Indians carried them off to tear them to pieces. The number of Indians pursuing us could have been about five or six thousand.

Quoted in Patricia de Fuentes, ed., *The Conquistadors: First-Person Accounts of the Conquest of Mexico.* Norman: University of Oklahoma Press, 1993, p. 155.

rows," by Spanish writers. More than six hundred Spaniards died in the retreat, along with many of their Indian allies. A number of those fleeing perished because they were weighted down with treasure, which they refused to leave behind. Also, more than two hundred other Spaniards had been stationed in a different part of the city and did not realize their comrades were trying to escape. These stragglers were captured. And they, along with others caught on the causeway, were sacrificed on an Aztec altar. Stripped naked, they were forced to eat mushrooms that made them have hallucinations; then they were led to the altar, where Aztec priests held them down and cut out their beating hearts. Meanwhile, Cortés and those of his company who had managed to make it to the shore hurried away and took refuge in Tlaxcala.

An Invisible Army

It appears that after chasing the Spaniards out of Tenochtitlán, its residents assumed that the outsiders were gone for good. They chose a new emperor—Cuitlahuac, one of several Aztec nobles who months before had advised Montezuma not to let the strangers enter Tenochtitlán. And they began to restore the bridges that had been dismantled in the fighting.

But the Aztecs' hopes of restoring their society to normalcy were premature and short-lived. They had no way of knowing that the Europeans had left behind an invisible army that was far more deadly than the one bearing crossbows and guns. Unbeknownst to people on both sides, on arrival in Mexico one or more Spaniards had been carrying smallpox germs. And some of the natives had become infected. The disease soon spread with frightening rapidity through a population lacking any natural resistance to it. According to a surviving native account:

[The plague] lasted for seventy days, striking everywhere in the city and killing a vast number of our people. Sores erupted on our faces, our breasts, our bellies. We were covered with agonizing sores from head to foot. The illness was so dreadful that no one could walk or move. The sick were so utterly helpless that they could only lie on their beds like corpses. . . . A great many died from this plague, and many others died of hunger. They could not get up to search for food, and everyone else was too sick to care for them, so they starved to death in their beds.[31]

The plague inflicted not only terrible physical effects, but also crippling social and psychological ones, as one modern observer points out: "As so often happens when pestilence devastates a population, the side effects can be shattering, too. Belief in social norms breaks down. The fields are not cultivated. The harvest is left to rot. . . . People are paralyzed and lapse into stunned inaction. [Also] in the short term people lose the will to rebuild."[32]

Tenochtitlán Under Siege

While the plague was wreaking havoc in the heart of the Aztec empire, Cortés wasted no time in regrouping his army. Several hundred Spanish reinforcements arrived from Cuba. And upwards of ten thousand Tlaxcalans and other Indians gathered to help him defeat the already crippled Aztecs. In addition, Cortés's carpenters, aided by many Spaniards and natives, built a fleet of small ships. They then disassembled them and carted them in sections overland to Lake Texcoco; there, once reassembled, they would give the invaders control of the great waterway.

The new army marched on Tenochtitlán in December 1520. Throughout the siege, which lasted eighty days, the Aztec defenders displayed great valor as they fought for their homes and way of life. But ultimately, the attackers had overwhelming advantages. Because they controlled the lake, they could keep the city from receiving food and water. Also, the Spaniards, who had grown up in a land filled with walled towns, knew much about siege warfare. In addition, they had cannons, which could demolish a city's sturdiest structures.

As a result, after numerous battles and other struggles the Aztecs on the island saw no other choice but surrender. Cuitlahuac crossed the lake in a canoe and gave himself up to the Spaniards. Rather than treat his defeated enemy with mercy and dignity, however, Cortés tortured him in hope of finding the location of more gold and then brutally killed him. Meanwhile,

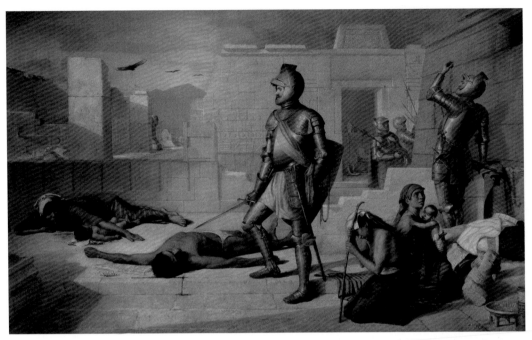

Aztecs in Tenochtitlán succumb to the Spaniards, who regrouped to attack the city once again in December 1520, beginning a lengthy siege that ultimately brought an end to the Aztec empire.

thousands of refugees poured out of the captured city. One eyewitness account says: "Everyone was in tatters. . . . The Christians searched all the refugees. They even opened the women's skirts and blouses and felt everywhere."[33]

"We Lie in Ruins"

After the fall of Tenochtitlán, the Aztec empire, which had been controlled through that city, virtually ceased to exist. Cortés was pleased to find that the major part of the conquest of Mexico had been accomplished. A couple of native towns offered some resistance, but most others "surrendered peaceably,"[34] in Aguilar's words. Wasting no time, Cortés then proceeded to make himself governor of Mexico. And using this author-ity, he allotted land parcels to his fellow conquistadors as well as to many of the Spanish settlers who began pouring into the region. Aguilar continues:

He sent some men with Pedro de Alvarado to settle the land of Oaxaca [south of Tenochtitlán], where he settled a city [and] gave the soldiers allotments of land. [Cortés] also sent Gonzalo de Sandoval, an excellent captain, with certain men to settle the land called Medellin [named for Cortés's hometown], where a good hundred allotments were made. . . . The rest of the soldiers who remained received allotments in Mexico [i.e., Tenochtitlán and its immediate surroundings].[35]

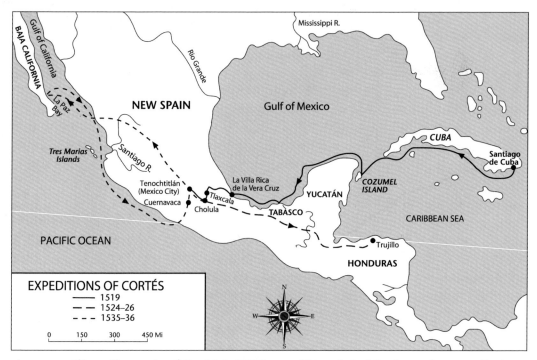

A map outlines the route of Cortés's 1519 expedition into Mexico, a journey that began in Cuba and ended with the defeat of the Aztec empire in Tenochtitlán, as well as his later treks through the region.

Cortés and most of his men felt no remorse for their naked conquest and the large-scale death and suffering it had brought about. They lived in a world in which the strong were expected to prey on, overpower, and rule the weak. They also believed that God was squarely on their side and wanted them to conquer the natives and force Christianity on them.

Ironically, the Aztecs had long held similar beliefs. They, too, had overcome weaker peoples by conquest. What they had not foreseen was that they might encounter invaders even more ruthless and brutal than themselves. Also like the Spanish, the Aztecs attributed the outcome of the war to divine forces. "You, the Giver of Life, you have ordained it [the Aztecs' fall]," an Aztec poet wrote shortly after the conquest. "We are crushed to the ground," he went on. "We lie in ruins. There is nothing but grief and suffering in Mexico . . . where once we saw beauty and valor."[36]

Chapter Four

Spanish and Native Armies

Historians and other observers have long marveled at how quickly Hernán Cortés and his tiny army were able to topple the Aztec empire. After all, that Central American realm contained millions of people and tens of thousands of well-armed warriors. This same scenario was later repeated in Peru, in South America, when another famous conquistador, Francisco Pizarro, conquered the Inca empire in short order. How did a few hundred Europeans bring entire empires to their knees so swiftly?

One commonly cited explanation is that the Spanish overcame the native armies through the battlefield use of guns. These were of two types—cannons, or artillery, and handheld guns called arquebuses. But modern historians do not put much stock in this argument. The fact is that the conquistadors' armies did not have many cannons and arquebuses. Cortés had fewer than twenty cannons,

for instance. And in most of the battles he fought with the natives, he had no more than a couple of dozen men armed with arquebuses. So from a tactical standpoint—that is, the number of warriors actually killed by these weapons—they had little effect against the Aztecs, Incas, and other natives.

However, the Spanish cannons did have a potent psychological effect, most often when fired in demonstrations staged to impress and scare the Indians. A native account of the war between the Aztecs and Cortés includes a description of the fear generated when his men first demonstrated one of their cannons in Tenochtitlán: "[The firing of the cannon] caused great confusion in the city. The people scattered in every direction. They fled without rhyme or reason. They ran off as if they were being pursued. . . . They were all overcome by terror, as if their hearts had fainted. And when night fell, the panic spread through the city."[37]

True, over time the Aztecs and other Indians got used to the conquistadors' cannons and lost their initial fear of them. However, by the time this happened it was too late. A combination of nonmilitary factors had already taken a terrible toll. These included diseases introduced by the newcomers that killed millions of natives; the Spaniards' political tactic of pitting some natives against others; and the effective use of deceit and surprise by Cortés and other conquistadors, who repeatedly took advantage of the natives' honesty, trust, and sense of honor and fairness.

Indeed, without these factors the Spanish conquests may well have failed. Or at least they may have taken much longer, perhaps decades or even generations. As the following examination of European and native weapons shows, with the exception of steel technology the opposing armies were more or less evenly matched in weaponry.

The Steel Advantage

It has been established that the tiny number of cannons and handheld guns possessed by the conquistadors made firearm technology a minor factor in their initial American conquests. In contrast, European steel technology proved to be a more significant advantage for the invaders. The Aztecs were unfamiliar with iron and steel (a harder version of iron made by adding charcoal to hot iron). They used other metals, including gold and silver for decoration and jewelry and copper and bronze (an alloy of copper and tin) for tools. But these met-

A conquistador is equipped with various armaments made from steel, including a helmet, an arquebus (firearm), a sword, and body armor.

als were softer and far less formidable than iron and steel. And the Europeans had learned to apply both iron and steel to warfare in numerous ways.

One of the more effective of these applications was the Spanish sword of that era. The steel making up its blade, forged in Toledo, Spain, was the finest in all of Europe. It was a full three feet (0.9m) long and double-edged, each edge being razor sharp. Another factor that made the sword lethal was that the Spanish soldiers who wielded it were well trained in slicing and hacking motions that could sever a person's arm in a single blow. Such swords were even more lethal in the hands of horsemen, who had the advantage of height and speed when attacking foot soldiers. Many Aztecs and other Indians were slain by the effective combination of steel swords and horses.

Another steel weapon the natives had never before encountered was the halberd, or poleax. It consisted of a long wooden handle topped by a steel blade that was part ax and part spear point. A soldier either jabbed the point to penetrate an opponent's armor or swung the ax portion back and forth with two hands. A single well-placed stroke of this weapon could bring down a horse and its rider. Scholar Albert Marrin adds that "a strong man swinging a halberd became a human buzz-saw, mowing down anyone in his path."[38]

The Spanish also used iron and steel to make various kinds of armor, which was tough enough to deflect most incoming arrows and sword blows. The Spanish soldiers, Marrin writes, "gleamed in polished steel helmets, breastplates, and arm pieces. Horses wore large . . . steel face masks."[39] When the Aztec emperor Montezuma's messengers first beheld such armor, which they learned was called "iron," they were duly impressed. They reported back to their master: "Their trappings and arms are all made of iron. They dress in iron and wear iron [helmets] on their heads. Their swords are iron. Their bows are iron [a reference to the iron bolts shot by crossbows]. Their shields are iron. Their spears are iron. . . . The strangers' bodies are completely covered, so that only their faces can be seen."[40]

Spanish Firepower

The natives were also impressed, at least at first, with the newcomers' firearms. The largest, the cannons, were fairly new to Europe's arsenals, as the earliest versions had appeared in the 1320s. And these had been so crude that they had had very limited military value. Because they had been fashioned of copper or brass, both soft metals, they tended to rip apart after only a few firings. They were also very inaccurate.

In the decades that followed, however, cannon technology quickly advanced. By the late 1300s gun makers were casting these weapons from iron, making them stronger and more reliable, and loading them with heavy iron cannonballs. In the 1400s European armies increasingly employed cannons to demolish the stone walls of castles and fortified towns. Another important breakthrough occurred shortly after 1450, when armies began mounting cannons on two-wheeled, horse-drawn carriages. This made artillery more mobile.

Mobility was essential to conquistadors like Cortés, who had to move their artillery through jungles, deserts, and rugged mountain passes. But because

Although their ability to wreak destruction was limited, the small cannons used by Spanish conquistadors were most effective in frightening the Indians, who were shocked by their flash and noise.

his cannons were small and few in number, their potential for sheer physical destruction was limited. Their main usefulness, Cortés found, lay in their initial shock value, because the natives had never before beheld such devices. Montezuma's messengers gave him the following description of the Spanish cannons: "A thing like a ball of stone comes out of its entrails. It comes out shooting sparks and raining fire. The smoke that comes out with it has a [terrible] odor, like that of rotten mud. The odor penetrates even to the brain and causes the greatest discomfort."[41]

The handheld arquebuses wielded by the Spaniards were also few in number and useful mainly for their shock value. They were essentially "matchlocks," because the operator ignited a small pan of gunpowder with a "match," a piece of smoldering rope. The resulting flash then penetrated a hole in the barrel and ignited more gunpowder inside. That explosion sent a metal ball flying out of the barrel.

Arquebuses were not very accurate. As military historian Archer Jones points out, "the gunner had about a fifty-fifty chance of hitting a line of men standing shoulder to shoulder about 100 yards away."[42] In fact, an arquebus was far less accurate than a crossbow. However, these guns were cheaper to make than crossbows and required much less skill and training to use. Moreover, the smoke and loud noise emitted by this firearm was initially scary to enemies unfamiliar with the weapon. For that reason the mere handful of arquebuses the Spaniards brought to the Americas made a big impression.

The Deadly Atlatl

It is important to emphasize that, after the initial novelty and shock of the European guns wore off, the Aztecs and other Native Americans were not greatly outmatched in weaponry. Native bows and slings were far more accurate and deadly than arquebuses, for example. In fact, the Aztecs, Incas, and other peoples of Central and South America possessed a wide array of effective weapons and were extremely skilled in their use.

One of the oldest, most reliable, and most lethal of these weapons was the atlatl, used by all of the Indians the conquistadors encountered. (Atlatl is the Aztec name for the weapon. Other Indians and early native peoples around the world had their own names for it, but modern scholars came to apply the Aztec term to all versions.) It was a throwing stick that was most often about 18 inches (45cm) long. It consisted of a wooden handle attached to a wooden socket or groove, into which the operator inserted a dart or short spear.

The hunter or warrior fired the dart by flipping the stick in a forceful overhand

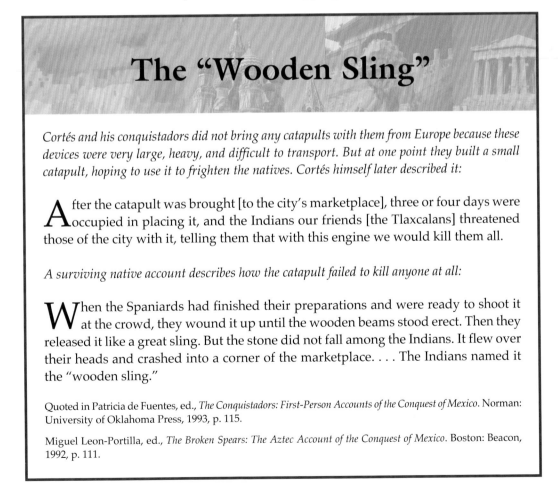

The "Wooden Sling"

Cortés and his conquistadors did not bring any catapults with them from Europe because these devices were very large, heavy, and difficult to transport. But at one point they built a small catapult, hoping to use it to frighten the natives. Cortés himself later described it:

After the catapult was brought [to the city's marketplace], three or four days were occupied in placing it, and the Indians our friends [the Tlaxcalans] threatened those of the city with it, telling them that with this engine we would kill them all.

A surviving native account describes how the catapult failed to kill anyone at all:

When the Spaniards had finished their preparations and were ready to shoot it at the crowd, they wound it up until the wooden beams stood erect. Then they released it like a great sling. But the stone did not fall among the Indians. It flew over their heads and crashed into a corner of the marketplace. . . . The Indians named it the "wooden sling."

Quoted in Patricia de Fuentes, ed., *The Conquistadors: First-Person Accounts of the Conquest of Mexico.* Norman: University of Oklahoma Press, 1993, p. 115.

Miguel Leon-Portilla, ed., *The Broken Spears: The Aztec Account of the Conquest of Mexico.* Boston: Beacon, 1992, p. 111.

A sculpture illustrates a grip on an atlatl, a throwing stick used by Indian warriors and hunters.

motion. In a sense, the atlatl became a fourth joint in the thrower's arm (the other three being the shoulder, elbow, and wrist), which imparted to the spear considerably more forward momentum than was possible using the arm alone. Another benefit was that one could fire the atlatl with one hand; in contrast, firing a bow required two hands. That meant a person could fire an atlatl with one arm while helping a wounded comrade with the other.

Another reason the atlatl was effective was that the Indians learned to use it at a young age and practiced almost daily for years. A combination of mechanical force and accuracy made this a very deadly weapon. In fact, many Spaniards were as awed by it as the natives were by Spanish cannons. One of the men who accompanied conquistador Hernando de Soto to North America in the 1540s later reported: "Our Spaniards had never seen this weapon before. [It] is capable of sending a dart with such great force that it has been seen to pass completely through a man armed with a coat of [armor]. In Peru, the Spaniards feared this weapon more than any others the Indian possessed."[43]

Native Swords, Shields, and Armor

Because the atlatl fired a kind of missile, it can be classified as a missile weapon. The Aztecs and other Indians had other missile weapons, including the bow and various kinds of slings, that had a greater range than the atlatl. Inca slings, which fired smooth stones about the size of chickens' eggs, were particularly lethal devices. According to a Spanish eyewitness: "They can hurl a [stone] with enough force to kill a horse. Its effect is almost as great as [a shot from] an arquebus. I have seen a stone shot from a sling break a sword in two when it was held in a man's hand thirty yards away."[44]

Native warriors also wielded swords. Although they were not as effective overall as Spanish ones, which had steel blades, the Indians' swords were nevertheless very dangerous on the battlefield. No matter what a sword is made of, much of its effectiveness depends on the skill of the user. Thus, a highly skilled native swordsman was at least an even match for a Spanish swordsman with an iron sword but only average fighting abilities. The principal sword used by the Aztecs was the *maquauhuitl.*

An Aztec warrior's shield, made of agave paper, leather, and reeds, is adorned with gold, feathers, and drawings.

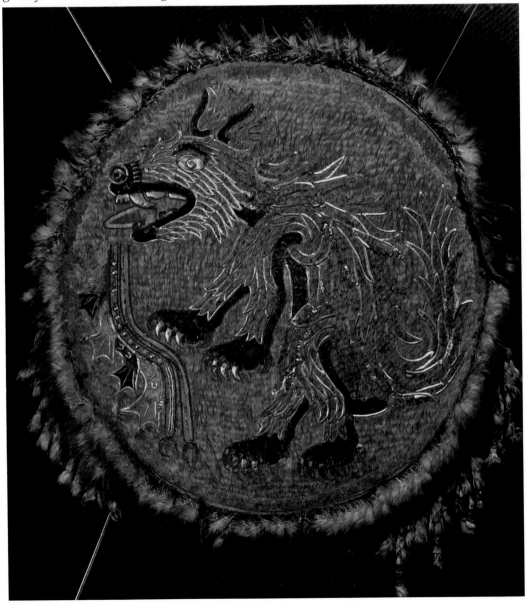

It consisted of a sturdy wooden club having grooves on its sides, into which razor-sharp slices of stone (usually obsidian) were wedged. One of the conquistadors in Cortés's army writes: "One day an Indian [armed with a native sword, whom] I saw in combat with a mounted horseman struck the horse in the chest, cutting through to the inside and killing the horse on the spot. On the same day, I saw another Indian give a horse a sword thrust in the neck that laid the horse dead at his feet."[45] The same Spaniard also describes the shields that Aztec warriors used along with their swords: "They carry shields of various kinds made of strong, solid cane woven with heavy double cotton, and decorated with feathers and round plaques of gold. The shields are so strong that only a good crossbow can shoot through them, but arrows [from an ordinary bow] do not damage them."[46]

Soldiers in the armies of the Aztecs, Incas, and most other native groups did not rely only on their weapons and shields. A common misconception today is that these Indians fought naked or almost so. In reality, they routinely wore armor, including helmets, that afforded a considerable amount of protection. A Spanish account of Aztec

Trials of an Aztec Warrior

Scholar Albert Marrin describes some of the customs surrounding Aztec warriors and their training:

The older boys fought alongside warriors assigned to look after them. The only way for an Aztec boy to become a man, and thus a full citizen, was to capture an enemy warrior for sacrifice. Killing him brought no honor, for the gods needed only the blood of the living. . . . A boy's head was shaved except for a pigtail that hung down the back. The pigtail was an insult to any spirited youngster, an announcement that he was still a child. Only a warrior who had taken a prisoner could cut off his pigtail. If he fought in three battles and still had his pigtail, anyone could insult him without fear of the law. . . . Success in battle was the only way for a commoner to rise in the world. Warriors received no pay, but those who took prisoners were rewarded by the tribe. The more prisoners he took, the more land and booty he received. This system of reward-by-merit made it possible for a slave's son to become a general, ambassador, [or] tax collector.

Albert Marrin, *Aztecs and Spaniards: Cortes and the Conquest of Mexico.* New York: Atheneum, 1986, p. 52.

armor of the conquistador era reads in part:

> The armor they use in warfare [is made] of quilted cotton the thickness of a finger and a half and sometimes two fingers, which is very strong. Over these they wear suits all of one piece and of a heavy cloth, which they tie in the back. These are covered with feathers of different colors. . . . The strength of their feathered garments is proportionate to their weapons, so that they resist spears and arrows, and even the sword. To defend the head, they wear [helmets] of wood, covered on the outside with feathers [or] gold or precious stones, and are something wonderful to see.[47]

"An Impressive Sight"

The combination of atlatls, bows, slings, swords, shields, and armor, most of these items colorfully decorated, was an impressive sight, especially when thousands of warriors marched into battle. The Spanish historian Francisco Lopez de Gomara, a contemporary of Cortés, describes the native army that confronted Cortés and his men when they first entered Tlaxcalan territory in September 1519:

> The men were splendidly armed in their fashion and their faces were painted with red [body paint], which gave them the look of devils. They carried plumes and maneuvered marvelously well. Their weapons

A portrait of Montezuma illustrates the colorful armaments of Aztec warriors, whose adornments created a spectacular and impressive sight when troops marched en masse into battle.

were slings, pikes, lances, swords, and bows and arrows; helmets; arm and leg armor of wood, gilded or covered with feathers or leather. Their breastplates were of cotton. Their shields [which were] very handsome and not at all weak, were of tough wood and leather, with brass and feather ornaments. Their

Respect for Aztec Warriors

Several of Cortés's men later wrote accounts of their experiences in Mexico. One of these narratives was published in the late 1500s in Italy, but by that time the identity of the author was lost. Ever since, he has been known as the "anonymous conquistador." In this passage he describes the fierceness of the native warriors, emphasizing that the Spaniards respected and sometimes feared them:

During combat they sing and dance and sometimes give the wildest shouts and whistles imaginable, especially when they know they have the advantage. Anyone facing them for the first time can be terrified by their screams and their ferocity. In warfare they are the most cruel people to be found, for they spare neither brothers, relatives, friends, nor women, even if they are beautiful. . . . When they cannot take the enemy plunder and booty with them, they burn everything.

Quoted in Patricia de Fuentes, ed., *The Conquistadors: First-Person Accounts of the Conquest of Mexico.* Norman: University of Oklahoma Press, 1993, p. 169.

swords [were] of wood with [pieces of sharpened] flint set into them, which cut well and made a nasty wound. Their troops were arranged in squadrons, each with many trumpets, conches [seashells], and drums, all of which was a sight to see.[48]

All of these Spanish accounts of native arms have a common thread running through them. Namely, those who wrote them were highly impressed by the Indian armies they witnessed, including the warriors' weapons, fighting skills, discipline, and bravery. The often-repeated modern notion that the conquistadors possessed vastly superior weapons and courage, with which they easily defeated the Indians, is incorrect. At several points in their conquests, the Spanish came perilously close to being annihilated. This was certainly the case with Pizarro and other conquistadors in South America. During one of the most fateful conquests in world history, they hovered at the very brink of doom before successfully overcoming incredible odds.

Chapter Five

Subjugation of the Incas

During the years in which Cortés was conquering the Aztec empire in Mexico, he and other Europeans had little knowledge of the vast lands that stretched north and south of that region. They did know that a large island or continent lay to the south. Several years before, in 1500, two expeditions had reached the eastern coast of that land mass. One was led by Spaniard Vicente Pinzón; the other was under the command of Portugal's Pedro Álvares Cabral. But for a generation or more after that, no large-scale European explorations of South America took place. So almost nothing was known about its size, terrain, climate, and inhabitants.

Therefore, the Spanish conquerors of Central America did not realize that a native empire even larger than the Aztec one covered parts of what are now Peru, Ecuador, Colombia, Bolivia, and Chile. This was the Inca realm. Like *Aztec*, the term *Inca* is a misnomer. The Spanish and other Europeans came to call the native inhabitants the Incas, which remains standard usage today. However, for those natives the term *Inca* denoted only their ruler. They called themselves the Tawantinsuyo and their empire Tawantinsuyu, the "Land of the Four Quarters."

At its height, the Inca empire, which the Spaniards came to call Peru, was huge even by the standard of European empires. If superimposed on a map of Europe, it would stretch from Spain in the west to the Russian steppes in the east. The Inca realm covered approximately 792,000 square miles (2 million sq. km) and had a population of somewhere between 9 and 20 million. (At the time, Spain's population was only about 6 million.) Moreover, the Inca empire was efficiently maintained, partly because it had a large network of roads connecting its many towns and cities. This allowed messengers, administrators, and soldiers

The Inca Empire

The Inca Empire

Land above 2,000 meters

COLOMBIA

ECUADOR

Rio Cenapa

Tumbes

Rio Napo

Iquitos

Rio Marañon

Amazon River

BRAZIL

Piura

Rio Ucayau

Chiclayo

Trujillo
Caraz
Chimbote
Sechin

Pucallpa

▲ Huascaran

PERU

THE

PACIFIC OCEAN

Huancayo

Lima ✪
Ayagucho

Machu Picchu
Cuzco

Pisco

ANDES

Ica
Nazca

BOLIVIA

Puno

Lake Titicaca

Arequipa

Desaguadero

N

Tacna

CHILE

0   200 km

to reach any part of the realm fairly quickly. It also had an extensive system of food storehouses. The government ordered farmers to place a percentage of their crops in these depots to create a surplus for use if harvests were poor or famine struck.

Despite the size, efficiency, and prosperity of their empire, however, the Incas were unable to withstand the catastrophe created by the arrival of the Spanish conquistadors. The newcomers were few in number. But they brought with them crippling diseases and an extraordinary ability to play one native group against another. In only a few short years they decimated the Inca population and reduced the survivors to virtual slaves in one of Europe's most profitable overseas colonies.

Tales of a Wealthy Kingdom

The key figure among the conquistadors who went to Peru was Francisco Pizarro. Born circa 1471 in the same region of Spain from which Cortés hailed (and a distant relative of Cortés's), Pizarro traveled to Spain's New World colonies in 1502. Eleven years later he served as a senior officer to Vasco Núñez de Balboa. The members of Balboa's expedition traversed Panama and were the first Europeans to see the Pacific Ocean. When Panama officially became a Spanish colony in 1518, Pizarro settled down there as a planter and swiftly acquired wealth and high social position.

In the years that followed, Spaniards from Panama began exploring the unknown lands lying farther south. In 1522 Pascal de Andagoya made it to the coast of what is now Colombia. Some local natives told him about a wealthy kingdom lying still farther south near a river called the Piru (which the Spanish corrupted to "Peru"). Returning to Panama, Andagoya stimulated avid interest among other leading colonists. Hoping to find and exploit the rich native kingdom, in 1524 Pizarro and a financial partner, Diego de Almagro, mounted a small expedition consisting of about eighty men. But the group made it no farther than northern Colombia. There, bad weather, lack of

food, and wounds acquired in skirmishes with the natives forced the adventurers to return to Panama.

Pizarro and Almagro launched their second expedition in November 1526. They reached the mouth of the San Juan River in Colombia, where Pizarro remained while Almagro returned to Panama to acquire reinforcements. Meanwhile, Pizarro's navigator, Bartolomé Ruiz, sailed farther south. Ruiz soon encountered a large, well-built boat manned by twenty Indians. The vessel contained not only valuable gold and silver items, one historian writes, but also "finely woven cloth embroidered with

Spanish conquistador Francisco Pizarro was part of an expedition led by Vasco Núñez de Balboa before he decided to launch his own expeditions, which eventually led him to the Inca empire.

birds and flowers" and "two Peruvians from the Inca port of Tumbes." Their stories of "palaces sheeted with gold and silver"[49] excited Ruiz. He hurried back to Pizarro, who was eager to press on down the coast.

However, because of various difficulties, including a long wait for badly needed supplies from Panama, Pizarro was unable to reach Tumbes until April 1528. There, he met with the local Inca governor. This official welcomed the strangers and gave them a tour of the town, which had many large, finely constructed buildings. He also showed them the nearby extensive farms and irrigation canals. The Spaniards were amazed at how civilized and sophisticated the Indians were.

Pizarro learned that Tumbes was a mere outpost on the fringes of a vast kingdom. It was clear that he would need more men and equipment than he then possessed to conquer that realm. So he left two of his men behind to learn the local language and returned to Panama.

Pizarro stands before King Charles V of Spain, who granted permission for him to invade and conquer Peru, provided that he share the spoils with the Spanish government.

An Indian's View of the Conquest

Waman (or Guaman) Poma was a Peruvian Indian born not long after Francisco Pizzaro's conquest of the region. As a young man, Poma became fluent in Spanish and eventually became a writer. Drawing on testimony from elderly people who remembered the conquest, he described it from the natives' point of view. In this passage he reconstructs some of the initial conversation between Pizarro and Atahuallpa in Cajamarca's town square just before the Spaniards attacked the assembled natives:

[Pizarro] told him he was the messenger and ambassador of a great lord and that he should be his friend and that he had come only for this. He [Atahuallpa] responded very politely to what Don Francisco Pizarro had said and the interpreter Felipe the Indian translated. The Inca responded with majesty and said that it was true that, having come as a messenger from so distant a land, he believed it must be a great lord, but that he did not have to make friendship, as he too was a great lord in his kingdom.

Quoted in Waman Poma, *The First New Chronicle and Good Government.* www-personal.umich.edu/~dfrye/guaman.htm.

From there he sailed to Spain to get more financial backers and the blessings of the Spanish king. Pizarro struck a deal with that ruler, Charles V, whereby Pizarro had the right to conquer and exploit the native kingdom as long as the Spanish government shared in the take.

Ascent into the Andes

On his return to Panama early in 1530, Pizarro brought with him many conquistadors, including his three half brothers, Gonzalo, Hernando, and Juan. He needed men he could trust. Also, he wanted his family to benefit as much as possible from the venture. In Michael Wood's words, "It was the beginning of the family's almost Mafia-like grip on the affairs of Peru, a private [business group] which grew from the original small company into a vast financial and military enterprise, linking the private interests of the Pizarros to the political ambitions of the Spanish empire."[50]

The new expedition, consisting of 180 men, departed Panama on December 27, 1530. For reasons that are now unclear, Pizarro took his time moving down the coast, stopping at one point in Ecuador for several months. Finally, the Spaniards arrived in Tumbes in April 1532.

To his surprise, Pizarro found the place in ruins and almost deserted. The few natives he met told him that the destruction had been the result of a civil war then still ongoing between two rivals for the Inca royal throne. Not long after the Spaniards' earlier visit, the locals explained, a terrible plague had struck the realm. It had killed the great Inca ruler Wayna (or Huayna) Capac, after which his sons, Atahuallpa and Huáscar, had begun fighting each other for supremacy.

At this point neither the Indians nor Spanish realized that the disease that had killed Wayna Capac was smallpox. Introduced by the Spanish in Mexico, where it had crippled the Aztecs, it had somehow spread southward and penetrated the Inca lands. Modern experts estimate that the disease killed at least 60 percent of the Inca realm's inhabitants in only a few years.

Pizarro was nothing less than thrilled by the news of the plague and civil war. He immediately realized that these events were fortunate for him because they had severely weakened the natives and, conversely, greatly increased the Spaniards' chances of success. To further tilt the odds in his favor, he enlisted the support of many local Indians—subjects of the Incas who hated their imperial masters.

Then the combined army of Spaniards and natives ascended into the nearby Andes mountains. Pizarro had heard that Atahuallpa was in the city of Cajamarca, which lay at an altitude of 13,500 feet (4,100m), and he was eager to confront him. The army reached Cajamarca in November 1532. One Spaniard describes the city this way:

The houses were more than two hundred paces in length, and very well built, being surrounded by strong walls three times the height of a man. . . . The interiors are divided into eight rooms, much better built than any we had seen before. The walls are of very well cut stones and each lodging . . . has its fountain of water in an open court, conveyed from a distance by pipes.[51]

From Arrogance to Mass Murder

Atahuallpa was bathing in some hot springs south of the town when the conquistadors arrived. The ruler greeted the strangers in a friendly manner. But they acted with coolness bordering on hostility toward him. Realizing that the Incas had never seen horses before, one of the Spaniards rode his steed right up to Atahuallpa's face, hoping to make him cower in fright. But the Inca prince held his ground and remained calm.

A much more eventful confrontation took place in the city's main square a couple of hours later. Having asked the newcomers to meet him there, Atahuallpa made a grand entrance. According to a Spanish eyewitness, the prince, accompanied by more than five thousand Incas, rode "in a very fine litter" that was decorated with silver. "Eighty lords carried him on their shoulders. [He] was very richly dressed, with his crown on his head and a collar of large emeralds around his neck. . . . Then came many men in squadrons, with headdresses of gold and silver."[52]

Stepping forward, Pizarro declared that he was the ambassador of a great king from across the sea who desired friendship with the Incas. But no sooner was this nicety spoken when a Spanish friar named Vicente stepped forward and arrogantly began demanding that the Indians renounce their own gods and bow to the Christian god.

One surviving account tells how the friar "told the Inca Atahualpa that he . . . should adore the cross and believe in the Gospel of God and not worship anything [else], that all the rest was mere mockery."[53]

The Inca ruler asked Vicente who had told him such a thing. And the friar answered that the Europeans' holy book, the Bible, had told him. Atahuallpa said: "Give me the book, so that it will tell me." And so he gave it to him and he took it in his hands and began to look through the pages of the book. And the Inca said: "Well, why doesn't

Inca leader Atahuallpa, accompanied by throngs of Inca warriors, leads a spectacular procession through the town of Cajamarca on his way to meet Pizarro.

it tell me? The book doesn't even talk to me!"[54] Atahuallpa then tossed the book onto the ground.

Shocked, Vicente screamed for the conquistadors to open fire on the crowd and:

> the knights began to fire their arquebuses [and] to kill Indians like ants. And [because] the plaza of Cajamarca [was] so full of Indians, the walls of the enclosure . . . came falling down, and people were killed between them. From being squeezed and being stepped on and trampled by the horses, many people died.[55]

At least two thousand Indians were slain in the massacre, and many more were wounded. The Spaniards also took some five thousand Incas captive, including Atahuallpa and members of his family. They chained the young ruler securely, cruelly winding one chain around his neck.

Atahuallpa's Fate

Almost immediately, the Spaniards began demanding that their prisoner give them gold. This no doubt seemed odd to him. As one modern observer points out: "Gold had an aesthetic [artistic] rather than a monetary value [to the Incas]. They used it for decorating their shrines, for the images of their gods, but not for bartering. They found the Spanish obsession for gold as a commodity uncouth and even uncivilized."[56]

Nevertheless, Atahuallpa believed that if he supplied the intruders with gold, they would be satisfied and go away. He struck a deal to that effect with Pizarro and then ordered messengers to go out and tell his people to gather large amounts of gold and give it to the Spaniards. Much of it came from Inca temples, which were richly decorated in gold. Having looted these houses of worship and defaced many magnificent works of art, Pizarro's men melted down the gold and recast it into bars.

But the Spaniards had no intention of keeping their side of the bargain. Not long after he had collected the bulk of the gold, Pizarro accused the Inca ruler of plotting against him and sentenced him to be burned alive. On July 26, 1533, Spanish guards took Atahuallpa to Cajamarca's main square and tied him to a stake. According to eyewitnesses: "The friar was, in the meantime, consoling him and instructing him through an interpreter in the articles of the Christian faith." Hoping he might be spared, Atahuallpa agreed to be baptized. But right after the friar administered the rites, they strangled the Inca with "a piece of rope that was tied around his neck." Then "some fire was thrown on him."[57]

The Great Inca Rebellion

At the time of Atahuallpa's execution, his rival brother Huáscar was already dead (having either died in battle or been assassinated by Atahuallpa's agents). That left the Incas without a native ruler. To further solidify his control over the populace, Pizarro placed another of Atahuallpa's brothers, Tupac Huallpa, on the throne. This young man

A captive Atahuallpa, tied to a stake, submits to a Christian baptism by a Spanish friar in hopes that his life will be spared; once the ceremony was complete, the ruthless Spaniards killed him anyway.

A Splendid Shrine Defaced

One Spaniard gave this description of the Temple of the Sun in Cuzco, the holiest temple in the entire Inca realm, before Pizarro's and Atahuallpa's men stripped it of its treasures in only a few days:

All of the [temple's] doors were covered with plaques of gold and the walls of the building were crowned on the outside with a gold band three feet wide that went all around it. [There were] five large square rooms . . . roofed over in the form of a pyramid. The first of these rooms was dedicated to the Moon, the bride of the Sun, [and] it was entirely paneled with silver and a likeness of the Moon with the face of a woman.

Quoted in Hammond Innes, *The Conquistadors*. New York: Knopf, 1969, p. 295.

died unexpectedly a few months later. So the Spaniards chose another puppet ruler, Manco Inca Yupanqui.

Manco started out supporting the occupiers in good faith, believing it would help his people. But over time he was treated shabbily by Pizarro's brothers and came to realize that he, too, was being used. So in 1536 Manco led a rebellion against the Spaniards. At first, he made some headway and in 1537 almost drove the Europeans from the Inca capital of Cuzco. But thanks to the arrival of reinforcements, they were able to maintain their hold on the city.

Manco retreated into the rugged mountains near Cuzco, where the Spaniards hunted for him for many years. They finally caught up with him in 1544. His son, Titu Cusi, who witnessed his death, later recalled:

My father [tried] to make some defense, [but] there were seven of them [Spanish assassins] with arms. He fell to the ground covered with wounds and they left him for dead. I was only a small boy [but] they turned furiously upon me and hurled a lance which only just failed to kill me also. I was terrified and fled among the bushes. They searched for me but failed to find me.[58]

A few other Incas stubbornly continued to resist until 1572, when their last stronghold was captured. Pizarro did not live to see this event. He died at the hands of the son of his former business partner, Almagro, the climax of a bitter feud between the two families.

The chain of events Pizarro had set in motion continued unabated, however. In the space of only a generation, an entire civilization was nearly swept away. And during these years the conquerors showed little or no regard for human rights, human life, or even the need to conserve precious resources for the future. As historian Hammond Innes puts it:

No provision was made for the maintenance of the advanced system of irrigation on which the country depended for its crops. The flocks of llamas [the mainstay of livestock in the region] were slaughtered in feast after feast without regard for the future. Wherever the Spaniards went, the story was one of looting, rape,

Incas round up gold and treasures at the command of the Spaniards, whose unscrupulous lust for wealth and fortune ultimately decimated the Inca empire.

The War with Manco Inca Yupanqui

During the years that the Spaniards hunted for Manco Inca and his followers, many skirmishes between the two groups occurred. In the book he wrote about the Incas, Pedro Cieza de León, a conquistador under Pizarro and later a historian, describes one of these incidents:

The Indians of Manco Inca could easily do great harm to the Spaniards and their allies, and in fact they killed and robbed many. The matter became so serious that [Pizarro] dispatched captains against them. [He] sent Captain Villadiego with a force [which] ascended a high sierra [in search of Manco]. And when they reached the top, they were so tired and exhausted that Manco Inca, with a little better than eighty Indians, fell upon the Spaniards [and] killed Captain Villadiego and all the others, save two or three who managed to escape.

Pedro Cieza de León, *The Incas*, trans. Harriet de Onis. Norman: University of Oklahoma Press, 1976, pp. 121–22.

and murder, and the profligate [reckless] waste of the carefully accumulated wealth of the Inca storehouses.[59]

Yet these enormous sums of treasure and supplies were still not enough for the invaders. Even before the fall of Manco Inca, some of the conquistadors set their sights on new conquests. Plunging headlong into the vast unknown territories lying east of the Andes, they unknowingly set in motion one of history's greatest voyages of adventure.

Chapter Six

Voyage Down the Amazon

In the initial centuries of European colonization of the Americas, one discovery or conquest often led to another. Thus, while conquering the Incas, the Spanish conquistadors began to hear tales from local Indians about a fabulous place called El Dorado. The name, meaning "the gilded one," was originally applied to a native king who supposedly ruled a vast kingdom somewhere in South America's interior. The records of sixteenth-century Spanish historian Gonzalo Fernández de Oviedo tell the legend this way:

> That great lord or monarch constantly goes about covered with gold ground [into dust] and as fine as ground salt. For it is his opinion that to wear any other adornment is less beautifying. . . . I would rather have the sweepings from the chamber of this monarch than that of the great melting establishments that

have been set up for [the refining of gold] in Peru.[60]

Many Spaniards in Peru came to believe that El Dorado was a real ruler, and they soon began calling his kingdom El Dorado, too.

One of the conquistadors who became infatuated by the legend was Francisco Pizarro's half brother Gonzalo. A dark-haired, muscular young man, Gonzalo Pizarro had the reputation of a skilled soldier and a highly motivated, determined individual. Also, thanks to his family's success in conquering and colonizing Peru, he was extremely rich. A partial list of his holdings included houses, shops, plantations, cattle ranches, and silver mines, as well as hundreds of Indian slaves. Many of these assets were concentrated in and around Quito, in the highlands of what is now Ecuador. (Founded in 1534 on the site of an Inca town that had burned the year before,

Attendants blow gold dust onto the body of the mythical El Dorado, whose vast riches were sought by Spaniards enticed by stories of his kingdom somewhere in the wilds of South America.

Quito quickly grew into one of the leading Spanish towns in the region.)

Pizarro had no desire to settle down and enjoy the comforts and luxuries he could now afford. He chose instead to use his wealth to accomplish three ambitious goals. One was to find El Dorado and exploit its riches. He also wanted to locate another fabulous place some of the Indians had spoken about—La Canela, the "Land of Cinnamon." Cinnamon was a highly coveted spice in Europe, so acquiring vast forests of cinnamon trees would be very profitable. Finally, Pizarro wanted to open up still more fertile territories to Spanish colonizers and settlers.

As it turned out, Gonzalo Pizarro's efforts to achieve these goals were doomed to failure. However, his expedition did end up serving an important purpose from a historical standpoint. It was the springboard for an epic journey of discovery by one of his lieutenants, conquistador Francisco de Orellana. A distant cousin of the Pizarros, Orellana became the first European to travel down the world's largest river (by volume)— the mighty Amazon.

Remote, Impassable Landscapes

In February 1541, when the expedition left Quito, none of its members had any inkling of the dangers and harrowing fight for survival that lay ahead of them. Indeed, Pizarro apparently felt that he had gathered more than enough personnel and supplies to achieve success. He had about 250 Spaniards, including many top-notch soldiers and several carpenters and construction workers. He also took along some four thousand Indians to serve as guides and laborers, more than two hundred horses, dozens of hunting dogs, tons of food and supplies, and more than two thousand hogs to provide fresh meat along the way. In addition, he included a Catholic friar, Gaspar de Carvajal, who kept a detailed written record of a large portion of the journey. It has survived and provides a vivid, at times gripping account of the incredible adventures that ensued.

From the start, the journey proved more difficult than expected. The countryside east of Quito was mountainous and extremely rugged and had no roads or footpaths to follow. Therefore, the travelers had to construct their own roads as they went, a slow, backbreaking endeavor. They were also hampered by heavy rains that at times went on for days without letup and soaked everyone to the skin.

At one point Pizarro took about seventy of his men on a side trip to the region where he hoped to find the Land of Cinnamon. After several weeks they did find some cinnamon trees. But they were small, few in number, of poor quality, and located in a very remote area that would not be profitable to settle and exploit. In a later letter addressed to the Spanish king, Pizarro explains:

> We found the trees which bear cinnamon, [and] neither the bark nor the rest [of the tree] has any flavor whatsoever. And these trees were on some mountainsides very rugged, unsettled, and uninhabitable, [and] some of the trees were small [and] they stood at long stretches from one another. It is a land and a commodity by which Your Majesty cannot be rendered any service or be benefited [because the cinnamon] is in small quantities and [would be a source] of even smaller profit.[61]

Pizarro pushed on, hoping that finding El Dorado would make up for the failure to find La Canela. However, after the passage of many weeks he found nothing but more remote, nearly impassable landscapes in which little food could be found. Eventually, the food his men had brought along began to run out. Also, most of the Indian servants died from a combination of brutal mistreatment, starvation, and European diseases.

Desperate for Food

In December 1541 the surviving Spaniards, still numbering more than two hundred, camped on the banks of a river (later determined to be the Upper

Coca). They were lost, hungry, and very discouraged. Moreover, several dozen men had been wounded during periodic attacks by local natives, who evidently did not appreciate intruders in their lands. Pizarro decided to build a boat to make it easier to transport the injured men and the remaining supplies. It was 26 feet (8m) long and 8 feet (2.4m) wide, and they christened it the *San Pedro.*

By Christmas, all of the original supplies were gone and the men were forced to start killing and eating their horses and dogs. At this point, Orellana approached Pizarro and offered to take the boat and a few men farther downriver to search for food. According to Carvajal's account, Orellana stated that "if luck favored him to the extent that he should find an inhabited region and foodstuffs . . . he would let him know about it, and that [Pizarro] should wait for him for three or four days, or as long as he should see fit. [Pizarro] told him to do whatever he thought was best."[62]

Orellana departed the day after Christmas with fifty-seven men, including Friar Carvajal. Soon the speed of the river unexpectedly and rapidly increased. And a mere three days into the mission it became clear that going back would be too difficult, if not impossible. Carvajal writes: "We did not find food for a [great] distance, [nor] were we finding

Orellana's trek down the Amazon, originally launched in a search for food to bring back to Gonzalo Pizarro's stranded party, soon became an expedition of its own.

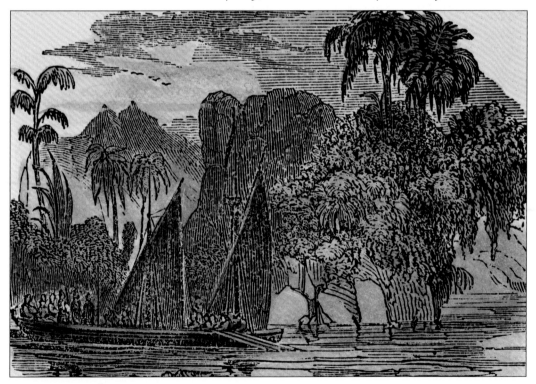

Pizarro's Version of Orellana's Departure

In his firsthand account, Friar Carvajal claims that Orellana departed in good faith, sincerely planning to find food and bring it back to Gonzalo Pizarro and his men. But no food was found. And eventually Orellana strayed too far to make returning practical. Pizarro saw it quite differently, however. In his letter penned later to the king, he bitterly states:

Being confident that captain Orellana would do as he said, because he was my lieutenant, I told him that I was pleased at the idea of his going for the food, and that he should see to it that he returned [and] and in no case went beyond the junction of the rivers [up ahead, and] give his attention to nothing else. [But] instead of bringing the food, he went down the river without making any arrangements [for the aid of me and my men, thus] displaying toward [the expedition] the greatest cruelty that ever faithless men have shown. [And] when I saw how Orellana had gone off and had become a rebel, I set about searching for the [food].

Gonzalo Pizarro, "Letter to the King, September 3, 1542," in Jose Toribio Medina, *The Discovery of the Amazon*, trans. H.C. Heaton. New York: AMS, 1970, pp. 248–49.

any [for ourselves], from which cause we suffered very great privation [hardship], and so we kept going on, beseeching Our Lord to see fit to guide us."[63]

This unfortunate turn of events left Gonzalo Pizarro and his men alone in the wilderness. Desperate for food, they ate lizards, snakes, and any other small animals they could catch. After a while, Pizarro sent one of his men, Gonzalo Pineda, to search for an inhabited village. Pineda was successful and returned with a large supply of cassava cultivated in a native field. But though this filled the men's stomachs, two died and many more became violently ill (because if not cooked properly, cassava is poisonous).

Despite these hardships the Spaniards marched on and ascended once more into the Andes. In June 1542, sixteen months after leaving Quito, they returned to that city exhausted and ragged but jubilant to be home. Pizarro later said: "At the cost of great suffering and with the loss of everything that we had taken along with us, we got back up to [Quito] with only our swords and each with a staff [wooden walking stick] in his hand. . . . From Quito to where I turned back must be more than 270 leagues [810 miles, or 1,304km]."[64]

"A Vast Fluid Wilderness"

Meanwhile, many miles away, huddled in the tiny *San Pedro*, Orellana and his

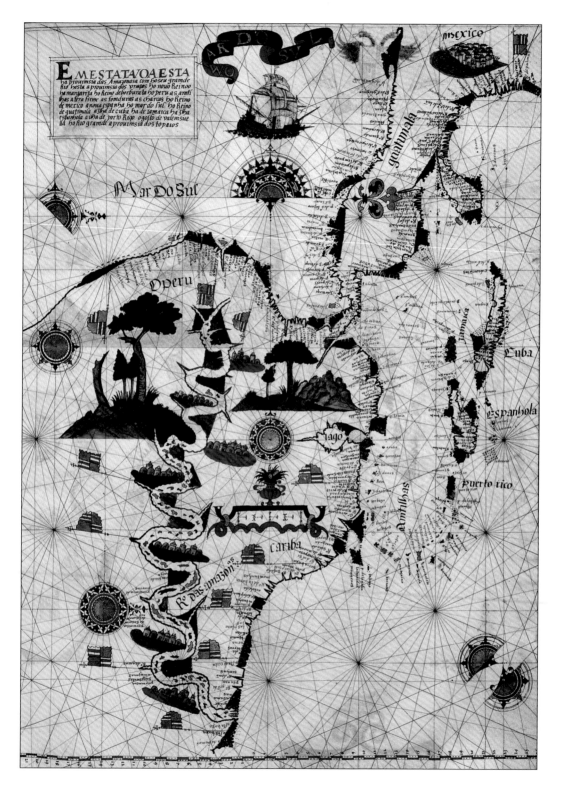

A sixteenth-century map of South America depicts the Amazon River winding through the continent before finally emptying into the Atlantic Ocean.

men continued their reluctant journey on an immense river that wound its way through dense rainforests never before seen by Europeans. "They were now on the main floor of the Amazon," Michael Wood says,

> heading eastwards through a vast fluid wilderness. . . . The jungle stretches in every direction. Huge oxbows [pieces of land nestled within the river's curves] lead nowhere. Giant tributaries flow in, bearing the debris of the forest. Islands of wreckage swirl past. New lakes glint in the low sun. Great floods leave their long brown scars gouged through the green forest.[65]

Near the end of February 1542, almost two months after separating from Pizarro's group, Orellana stopped in a land his men called Apaira, after the name of the local ruler. The natives were friendly and hospitable. This may have been partly because Orellana claimed the Spaniards were semidivine messengers. According to Carvajal:

> He told them [that] we were children of the Sun. [At this] the Indians marveled greatly and manifested great joy, taking us to be saints or celestial beings, because they worship the Sun and hold it to be their god. . . . They then told the Captain [Orellana] that

How the River Got Its Name

The term *Amazon* originally came from ancient Greek mythology. It refers to a legendary race of women warriors who supposedly attacked Athens. In the 1500s several Spanish and other European explorers claimed to have heard stories of a similar tribe of women living somewhere in the South American wilderness. In fact, Orellana and his men claimed that they actually fought with these women in what is now Brazil. Assuming that the Spaniards did not fabricate this claim, who were the long-haired warriors they encountered? One possibility is that the women of the tribe in question fought alongside their husbands and fathers. Another is that the Spaniards fought men with very long hair who from a distance they mistook for women. Whatever the true circumstances of the incident, it inspired people to call the waterway the Rio Amazonas, the "River of the Amazons," a name that stuck.

they were his [servants]. The Captain thanked them well and then ordered many things to be given [to him]. Not a single thing did the Captain ask for that they did not at once give him.[66]

Orellana wisely took advantage of the natives' generosity. The Spaniards stayed in Apaira for nearly two months, during which they constructed a bigger boat. The *Victoria*, as they called it, was only slightly longer than the *San Pedro* but a good deal wider and could accommodate eighteen oarsmen. "Such great haste was applied to the building of the [boat]," Carvajal writes, "that in thirty-five days it was constructed and launched, calked with cotton and tarred with pitch, all of which the Indians brought. . . . Great was the joy of our companions over having accomplished that thing which they so much desired to do."[67]

On April 24 Orellana and his followers climbed into their two vessels and took leave of Apaira. Not far downstream they came to the land of the Machiparo people. The countryside was so heavily populated that a single town stretched for more than 18 miles (29km) along the riverbank. But for a long time the Spaniards could not risk going ashore to get a better look because the inhabitants were extremely hostile. Over the course of more than 200 miles (322km), Orellana's boats came under attack numerous times. Carvajal describes some of these incidents in detail, including a passage that reads in part:

They were coming on with a great yell, playing on many drums and wooden trumpets, threatening us as if they were going to devour us. [They] kept coming closer, with their squadrons [of boats] formed to catch us in the center. . . . Our crossbowmen began to inflict some damage on the enemy [and] when it was seen [by] the Indians that so much damage was being done to them, they began to hold back, yet not showing any sign of cowardice [and] there kept coming to them many reinforcements. . . . There were many Indians on the water and on land and from all sides they gave us a hard fight.[68]

Eventually, the travelers managed to land near a small village and drive away its inhabitants. There, the Spaniards found a great deal of food and collected as much as they could carry, but it was impossible to rest because the villagers soon returned and attacked. Six of Orellana's men were wounded in this and some later skirmishes with the Machiparo.

The Sea at Last

Later, the reluctant explorers reached the land of a people called the Omagua. The Spaniards stopped several times to visit villages that had been temporarily abandoned because their residents were afraid of the strangers. In these settlements the visitors were amazed to find pottery of a quality equal to or greater

Highly Civilized Natives

The sixteenth-century Spanish historian Gonzalo Fernández de Oviedo gives this description of the highly civilized natives Orellana saw living in villages along the banks of the Amazon and its tributaries. (Most of these cultures no longer exist.)

They are a people of considerable foresight, and they keep provisions on hand until the time they take in the next harvest, and they have other [supplies] in lofts or on hurdles raised above the ground the height of a man, [and] they keep [in] there their maize [corn] and their biscuits, which they make out of maize and cassava mixed together or bound with paste, and a great deal of roasted fish [and] game meat. In their houses they use ornaments, and they have very pretty mats made out of palm-leaf, and earthenware [pottery] in large quantities and of a very good quality. They sleep in hammocks. The houses are well swept and clean and are built of wood and covered with straw.

Gonzalo Fernández de Oviedo, *History of the Indies*, excerpted in Jose Toribio Medina, *The Discovery of the Amazon*, trans. H.C. Heaton. New York: AMS, 1970, p. 398.

than any they had seen in Europe. "There was a villa," Friar Carvajal writes,

in which there was a great deal of porcelain ware of various makes, both jars and pitchers, very large . . . and other small pieces such as plates and bowls and candle-holders of this porcelain [that was] the best that has ever been seen in the world, for that of Malaga [a Spanish city known for its fine pottery] is not its equal. [The native pottery] is glazed and embellished with all colors [that are] so bright that they astonish.[69]

After many more adventures, in early June 1542 the travelers first noticed a slight rise and fall of water on the riverbanks, a side effect of ocean tides. Heartened, they moved on, and on August 6, realizing that the sea was very near, they stopped on a large island. There they used whatever materials they could find, including palm fibers and wood from local trees, to refit the boats and make them more seaworthy.

The pivotal, thrilling moment came on August 26. After their grueling, death-defying voyage down the river, they emerged into the Atlantic Ocean, having traveled thousands of miles over the course of eight months. From there, both boats safely made it another 1,200 miles (2,132km) to Spanish colonies lying near South America's

Gonzalo Pizarro is led to his execution after joining his fellow conquistadors in a failed revolt against Spanish authorities in Quito.

northern coast. Incredibly, forty-seven of the original fifty-seven Spaniards, including Orellana and Carvajal, had survived the ordeal.

The Lust for Gold Still Strong

For all their troubles, Orellana and Gonzalo Pizarro never enjoyed the fame that history accorded Hernán Cortés and Francisco Pizarro. This was in large degree because of circumstances beyond the control of the individuals involved. Spain was unable to claim the Amazonian lands that Orellana had explored because a treaty signed by Spain and Portugal years before had already awarded the Portuguese rights to these territories.

Orellana went back empty-handed to Spain and got married. But three years later he returned to the Amazon. There, after a storm wrecked his ship, he disappeared, never to be heard from again. His former comrade, Gonzalo Pizarro, fared no better. After returning to Quito he got involved in a civil war among the local conquistadors and ended up being captured and beheaded.

The fact that neither man found any evidence for El Dorado's existence did not dash all hopes that it might be a real place. Several later expeditions searched for that legendary realm. Long after Cortés, the Pizarros, and Orellana were in their graves, the lust for gold, land, and power remained strong among many Spaniards and other Europeans.

Chapter Seven

Cabeza de Vaca's Incredible Journey

Nearly all of the Spanish conquistadors played some kind of direct role in conquering the native peoples of the Americas. However, there were a few exceptions. And one of these men, Álvar Núñez Cabeza de Vaca, stands out as particularly exceptional. Unlike Cortés and the Pizarros, Cabeza de Vaca befriended and defended the natives instead of subjugating and brutalizing them. And his story emerges as one of the most enthralling and inspiring tales of human survival ever told.

The Narváez Expedition

Cabeza de Vaca was born sometime between 1490 and 1500 in Jerez, a city in the province of Cádiz in southern Spain. As a young man he traveled to the Americas and eventually joined up with Pánfilo de Narváez. It was Narváez who had led a force of soldiers into Mexico in 1520 to arrest Cortés and who had been

defeated and lost an eye in the process. In the years that followed, Narváez had managed to repair his reputation. And in 1527 he had secured permission from the Spanish government to lead an expedition into Florida. At the time, this was the name the Spanish used to denote the entire southeastern portion of what would later become the United States. Among the four hundred conquistadors under Narváez's command was Cabeza de Vaca, who acted as the expedition's treasurer.

The expedition reached Tampa Bay, on the western coast of the Florida peninsula, in the spring of 1528. At this point Narváez and Cabeza de Vaca, who apparently did not see eye to eye on much, got into a dispute over strategy. Narváez wanted to lead most of his men ashore and trek inland several miles while the ships sailed up the coast in a parallel course. But Cabeza de Vaca argued that this was not a good idea. In the thoughtful, fascinating account he wrote later, he recalls:

> I replied that it seemed to me in no way advisable to leave the ships until they were in a safe, occupied port. I told him to consider that . . . the horses would not be with us in case we needed them, and furthermore, we had no interpreter to make ourselves understood by the natives and would not be able to converse with them. Neither did we know what to expect from the land we were entering . . . nor in what part of it we were, and finally that we did not have the supplies [necessary for] each man for the journey.[70]

Narváez overruled his treasurer and took about three hundred of his men,

Narváez and his party arrive at the Gulf of Mexico in the spring of 1528 after trekking through the Florida peninsula.

including Cabeza de Vaca, ashore. They moved several miles inland and marched north. Because the land was very swampy, progress was slow and the travelers did not rendezvous with the ships at the time agreed on earlier. After waiting a while, the officer in charge of the vessels gave Narváez and his men up for lost and sailed away to Cuba.

Suddenly marooned with few supplies in an unfamiliar wilderness, Narváez and his officers debated about what to do. They decided to build five bargelike boats. On these they hoped to make it across the Gulf of Mexico to Vera Cruz or some other port in Spanish-controlled Mexico. But a number of factors worked against them. They had no precise idea of their position, for example, and lacked maps or navigation instruments. Moreover, they were unaware that strong northerly winds often whip southward from what is now Mississippi, pushing boats out to sea.

Not only did the barges encounter these winds, they also became separated from one another. Cabeza de Vaca remembers: "The north wind that blew offshore picked up so much that it drove us back to the high sea, without our being able to do anything about it. . . . We sailed for two more days, trying hard to reach the shore [and] by dawn the boats had been driven apart from each other."[71] After a while, the men in Cabeza de Vaca's barge caught sight of the raft carrying Narváez. When they asked their commander what they should do next, he told them that "each one should do the best he could to save himself, which is what he intended to do, and with this he went on his [way]."[72] (Soon afterward Narváez and those with him disappeared; probably they starved to death or drowned.)

The Isle of Misfortune

Cabeza de Vaca and his comrades drifted for four more days, subsisting on a handful of corn each per day. Finally, they were exhausted, starving, and expecting the worst. "Because we had been suffering so many days from hunger," Cabeza de Vaca writes, "and from the injuries we had received from the waves, the next day people began to break down, so that [many men] were so near dying that few remained conscious. Just five men could stay on their feet."[73]

All seemed lost. But then the castaways suddenly washed up on the shore of an island. It was about 15 to 20 miles (24 to 32km) long and, considering the circumstances they were in, they named it the "Isle of Misfortune." Today, most experts think it was Galveston Island, which lies not far off the coast of Texas.

The next morning three local Indians appeared on the beach and stared curiously at the bedraggled Spaniards. Soon many more natives came to gawk at the strange bearded visitors. The Indians could see that Cabeza de Vaca and his companions were hungry, and, communicating through sign language, they promised to bring food. True to their word, not long afterward they brought some fish, which the famished men happily devoured.

Cabeza de Vaca and his comrades find themselves shipwrecked on an island they termed the "Isle of Misfortune," which was likely off the coast of what is now Texas.

Feeling revitalized, the next day the Spaniards tried to launch the barge, hoping to continue down the coast to Mexico. But only a few hundred feet from the beach a huge wave reared up and struck them. Some men drowned and the rest limped ashore and collapsed onto the sand. After a while, the Indians reappeared. "Upon seeing the disaster we had suffered," Cabeza de Vaca writes, "the Indians sat down with us and began to weep out of compassion for our misfortune."[74] This heartfelt display amazed the conquistadors. They had come to accept the idea that the natives of the Americas were ignorant, unreasoning, unfeeling savages. Yet here they had encountered what seemed to be fellow human beings capable of pity, kindness, and generosity. The natives went so far as to take the strangers to their village and build a hut for them to rest in.

Days turned into weeks, and Cabeza de Vaca and his comrades ended up staying the winter with the inhabitants of the Isle of Misfortune. Because it was a particularly harsh winter, many people, natives and Spaniards alike, died. And by spring only fifteen of the eighty shipwrecked men remained alive.

Adventures in Texas

Because Cabeza de Vaca lived among the Indians for many months, he learned

Cabeza de Vaca Describes the Natives

In his account of his adventures, Cabeza de Vaca includes a detailed description of the people and customs on the Isle of Misfortune, probably Galveston Island. The passage reads in part:

The people we encountered there are tall and well-formed. They have no other weapons than bows and arrows, with which they are most dexterous [nimble]. The men pierce one of their nipples from side to side. . . . Through this hole they thrust a reed [as] thick as two fingers. They also perforate [pierce] their lower lip and insert a piece of cane in it as thin as half a finger. The women do the hard work. . . . Of all the people in the world, they most love their children and treat them best. Should the child of one happen to die, parents and relatives bewail [grieve] it, as does the whole settlement. . . . Their lodges are made of matting and built on oyster shells, on which they sleep in [animal] hides.

Álvar Núñez Cabeza de Vaca, *Chronicle of the Narváez Expedition*, trans. Fanny Bandelier. New York: Penguin, 2002, pp. 37–39.

their language. These natives were Karankawas, a tribe that once inhabited the region of southeastern Texas stretching from Galveston Island to Corpus Christi. None survive today. So it is fortunate that in his memoir Cabeza de Vaca describes them and records some of their customs.

Eventually, after thoroughly adopting Indian ways, Cabeza de Vaca decided to leave the island and explore the nearby mainland. He met and joined some other natives who belonged to a group of seminomadic peoples known as the Coahuiltecans. They lived mainly in south-central Texas. After learning their language, Cabeza de Vaca became a trader, bartering sea shells and other items from the coast with Indians who lived deeper in the interior of Texas. "I spent six years in this country," he later wrote, "alone with them and as naked as they were."[75]

During these years Cabeza de Vaca thought often about moving on to a neighboring region. But he did not want to leave his friend, Lope de Oviedo, who was still on the Isle of Misfortune. All the other Spaniards had either died or left the island, but Oviedo refused to go. "In order to get Oviedo out of there," Cabeza de Vaca says,

I went over to the island every year, entreating [begging] him to leave with me and go in search of Christians. [But] year after year he put it off to the following year. In the end

I got him to come, took him away, and carried him across the inlets and the four rivers on the coast, since he could not swim.[76]

To Cabeza de Vaca's dismay, however, Oviedo soon changed his mind and returned to the island. Fortunately for Cabeza de Vaca, his gloomy mood lifted when some Indians told him that some other Spaniards were living in a village several miles down the coast. He went there immediately and found three other survivors of the Narváez expedition—Alonso del Castillo, Andres Dorantes, and a dark-skinned Muslim named Estevanico. The four men decided they should continue the journey to Mexico they had begun several years before. They hoped to reach the Spanish port town of Pánuco.

The Healers
Because of various difficulties, Cabeza de Vaca and his three companions were unable to begin their trek until a year

Cabeza de Vaca's trek took him through the expanse of the Texas desert, where he lived among the native people for several years before continuing on to Mexico.

later in the spring of 1535. Although they were optimistic about their chances, they discovered that a number of obstacles stood in their way. One was the Rio Grande River, which was more than 700 feet (213m) wide at the point where they encountered it. They managed to get across, "with water up to our chests,"[77] in Cabeza de Vaca's words.

But soon afterward they saw the massive, craggy stone wall of the Sierra Madre peaks looming up ahead. The local Indians told them that there were only two ways around this barrier— either southward along the coast or inland toward the northwest. The natives advised the travelers not to take the coastal route because the Indians in that region were hostile and would surely kill them. So the four men turned inland, hoping to make a loop that would carry them around the mountains and into the Valley of Mexico.

That loop turned out to be much longer and more involved than the Spaniards had anticipated. For months they traveled northwestward, crossing the Rio Grande again, as well as many

Cabeza de Vaca's expedition benefited from the assistance of native companions, who helped the group navigate the desert and mountains of what is now the southwestern United States and northern Mexico. The group reached the Pacific Ocean in December 1535.

Able to Raise the Dead?

During his travels through Texas and northern Mexico, Cabeza de Vaca became known as a healer, though he later admitted that he did little more than pray over sick people. At one point he prayed for a man who appeared to be dead. Soon afterward the man woke up, and thereafter the Indians of the region believed that Cabeza de Vaca could raise the dead. As he tells it:

There were many people around [the dead man], weeping. [I] found [him] with his eyes rolled back, without [a] pulse, and with all the marks of death, at least it seemed so to me. . . . As best I could, I prayed to our Lord to restore him to health [then] made the sign of the cross and breathed on him many times. . . . [That night, his relatives] returned, saying that the dead man [had revived], risen from his bed, walked about, eaten, and talked to them. [This] caused great surprise and awe, and all over the land nothing else was spoken of. Everyone who heard about it came to see us so that we might cure them and bless their children.

Álvar Núñez Cabeza de Vaca, *Chronicle of the Narváez Expedition*, trans. Fanny Bandelier. New York: Penguin, 2002, p. 60.

other rivers. Word about them spread to native villages far ahead, and people traveled considerable distances to see the strangers. These pilgrimages were partly motivated by the belief that the Spaniards possessed special skills and powers. Living among the Karankawas on the Isle of Misfortune, Cabeza de Vaca had gained a reputation as a healer, though he had never claimed to be one. Now large numbers of sick Indians "came from far and wide to be cured,"[78] as he describes it. Apparently, the Spaniards did little more than pray over the pilgrims; the fact that some of them got well was evidently enough to confirm the rumors about the bearded strangers' powers.

The four men kept moving westward. And they eventually decided to head down Mexico's western coast and then turn inland toward Mexico City. In December 1535, accompanied by almost a hundred native companions, they descended from the mountains of western Mexico to the Pacific coast. From there they headed south.

From the Darkness Into the Light

Eventually, the travelers came upon four Spanish slavers, conquistadors who made a living by capturing natives and selling them in the then thriving slave trade. The sight of some gaunt, half-naked Spaniards surrounded by a large group of Indians startled the slavers. "They stared at me quite a while, speechless," Cabeza de Vaca later recalled. "Their surprise was so great that they could not find the words to ask me anything."[79]

Suddenly, to his horror, Cabeza de Vaca realized that these men were planning to enslave the Indians who had accompanied him. The slavers told the natives that Cabeza de Vaca was a Spaniard who had "gone astray for awhile," that the Spaniards were the "lords of the land," and that the Indians had no

A rare 1555 edition of Cabeza de Vaca's book, The Account *or* Chronicle of the Narváez Expedition, *provides vivid descriptions of his adventures and speaks to issues of human rights, personal growth, and tolerance.*

choice but to "obey and serve." The Indians refused to believe this. One of them stepped forward, called the slavers liars, and said that Cabeza de Vaca "cured the sick," while the Spaniards "killed those who were healthy." He added that Cabeza de Vaca "asked for nothing," whereas the Spaniards had "no other aim than to steal what they could."[80]

Cabeza de Vaca promptly went to see the slavers' commander and made a forceful case that his Indian friends should be left alone. The commander agreed, after which Cabeza de Vaca bade the natives a sad farewell and watched them depart for their homelands. He did not find out until later that he had been tricked. After he had left the area, the slavers caught up to the Indians and put them in chains.

From Mexico City, Cabeza de Vaca traveled to Veracruz and from that port sailed to Cuba. The following year (1538) he finally made it back to Spain. Several years later he wrote his now famous account of his adventures, which long had the title *Naufragios* (*Shipwreck*) in Spanish. Today's English translations are variously called *The Account* or *Chronicle of the Narváez Expedition.*

Although the story Cabeza de Vaca told did not involve conquests and the fall of a civilization, as those of most other conquistadors did, it is perhaps even more powerful and meaningful than theirs. This is because it speaks across the ages to the modern world. Many people today see it as a parable, or lesson, about human worth, human rights, and tolerance for those who are

Cabeza de Vaca's Sad Fate

Cabeza de Vaca emerges in modern histories not only as an important explorer of and writer about the Americas in his era, but also as something of a tragic character. His transformation from treasure-seeking conquistador to enlightened champion of Indian rights proved to be his undoing. After returning to Spain in 1538, he obtained a license from the king to take some ships to the Spanish colony in Paraguay and serve as its governor. The colonists were already exploiting and brutalizing the natives, a practice he tried to stop. He also came out strongly against enslaving the Indians. Most of the colonists saw him as a misguided do-gooder, or even as deranged, and rebelled, after which they put him in chains and sent him back to Spain. In the years that followed, his enemies falsely accused him of various crimes, and his legal battles pushed him deeply into debt. He died in poverty in 1558 or 1559, regretting that he could not return to the Americas and help alleviate the misery of the natives.

different. As Michael Wood puts it: "The moment when Cabeza de Vaca stares at the Spaniards and sees himself as he was eight years before—his Spanish conquistador self—the moment when he defends Indian rights by putting his own life on the line . . . this amazing story transcends its time. Like all the best fiction, it is a maturation story, a story of spiritual growth and change."[81]

Thus, most of the other conquistadors were men of their own era, an age when violence, greed, cruelty, and intolerance thrived as a matter of course. Through his extraordinary experiences, Cabeza de Vaca evolved beyond this primitive mind-set and in a sense became a modern person. Therefore, his incredible journey was not merely across mountains, rivers, and deserts, but also from the darkness into the light. Moreover, he was not the only Spaniard of his time to undergo this intellectual transformation. The man who came to be known as the "last conquistador" was destined to attain a similar enlightenment.

The Last Conquistador

In the span of only two generations, the Spanish conquistadors changed the world forever. They swept into the previously unknown Americas, and through the use of force and deceit, aided by deadly European diseases, they brought low those continents' most splendid native empires. These conquests set in motion an irresistible tide of events. In the centuries that followed, Spain and other European nations colonized nearly every portion of the Americas.

For a while the New World was an extension of the Old World. The Americas were seen mainly as lands to exploit economically, as rich sources of gold, sugar cane, tobacco, and other commodities for European markets. But as new generations grew up in the colonies, their members increasingly felt themselves, their needs, and their goals to be separate from those of the mother countries. So eventually most of the colonies declared their independence and became new countries. Several of them, including the United States, played key roles in shaping the modern world.

"All Humankind Is One"

It must always be remembered that these sweeping events occurred at a terrible cost in human misery. Millions of Native Americans were slaughtered and millions more were enslaved. Entire societies and ways of life were devastated or eradicated by invaders who viewed themselves as morally superior to the Indians. During the age of the conquistadors, only a few Spaniards and other Europeans believed that what their nations were doing was wrong and spoke out against the conquests. Bartolomé de Las Casas, who took part in the famous debate at Valladolid in 1550, speaks the loudest: "All the peoples of the world are human beings. They are rational beings. All possess understanding [and] the natural capacity or faculties [to] master the knowledge that they do not have. . . . And no one is born enlightened. . . . Thus, all humankind is one."[82]

These sentiments were unpopular, even radical when Las Casas expressed them. But they ring true today in a world increasingly guided by similar statements of human dignity and human rights in the founding documents of the leading democracies and the United Nations. Moreover, Las Casas was vindicated in other ways. In the fullness of time, his prophecy that Spain would lose its overseas empire came true with a vengeance. In the 1800s and 1900s, the vast global realm that the conquistadors and their immediate successors had carved out collapsed. And today Spain, once the richest, most powerful nation on Earth, is a small country of modest means and influence.

Keeping Past Events in Perspective

Of course, it is easy in hindsight to praise Las Casas and other thinkers who were ahead of their time and to condemn the conquistadors as arrogant and brutal thugs. Yet in examining the events of past eras, it is always vital to keep them in perspective. Most human beings are and have always been products of the ages and societies in which they were born. And it would be a mistake to judge the deeds of people raised in an unenlightened age by the standards of later, more enlightened times. Thus, all can agree that Cortés, the Pizarros, and most other conquistadors were violent individuals motivated by greed and intolerant beliefs. At the same time, one can understand that these men grew up in a world in which concepts such as conquest and the superiority of some races and religions over others were accepted norms.

In fact, understanding the brutish forces that shaped the conquistadors makes the few of their number who overcame these forces seem all the more exceptional and commendable. This is why the deeds and words of Cabeza de Vaca are so moving to people today. Unlike Las Casas, Cabeza de Vaca was not a deep thinker. It was through a series of wrenching, character-shaping experiences that this conquistador came to the same conclusions about human dignity that Las Casas did. And this has earned Cabeza de Vaca the admiration of posterity.

It is perhaps appropriate that another conquistador who came to question and regret what he and his country had done was the last of his breed. Mansio Serra de Leguizamón went to Peru in his teens, where he helped to destroy some of the last Inca strongholds. Only much later in life did Leguizamón see the error of his ways. The words of his will, written in 1589 when he was an old man on his deathbed, now seem like a fitting epitaph for all the conquistadors:

The motive that moves me to make this statement is the peace of my conscience [and] the guilt I share. For we have destroyed by our evil behavior such a [society] as was enjoyed by these natives. They were so free of crime and greed [and] when they discovered that we were thieves [and rapists], they despised us. . . . There is no more I can do to alleviate these injustices other than by my words, in which I beg God to pardon me, for I am moved to say this, seeing that I am the last to die of the conquistadors.[83]

Notes

Introduction: An Epic Conquest Reevaluated

1. Michael Wood, *Conquistadors*. Berkeley: University of California Press, 2000, pp. 12–13.
2. Juan Ginés de Sepúlveda, "Concerning the Just Causes of the War Against the Indians," Latin Library at Ad Fontes Academy. www.thelatinlibrary.com/imperialism/readings/sepulveda.html.
3. Bartolomé de Las Casas, *A Brief Account of the Destruction of the Indies*, Project Gutenberg, 2007. www.gutenberg.org/files/20321/20321-8.txt.
4. William H. Prescott, *History of the Conquest of Mexico* (1843; repr.). London: Folio Society, 1994, pp. 648–49.

Chapter One: Rise of the Spanish Empire

5. William H. McNeill, *The Rise of the West*. Chicago: University of Chicago Press, 1992, p. 628.
6. Quoted in Hugh Thomas, *Rivers of Gold: The Rise of the Spanish Empire*. New York: Random House, 2005, p. 28.
7. Christopher Columbus, "The Columbus Letter: Translation," University of Southern Maine. www.usm.maine.edu/~maps/columbus/translation.html.
8. Quoted in Thomas, *Rivers of Gold*, p. 233.
9. Quoted in Wood, *Conquistadors*, p. 17.
10. Quoted in Thomas, *Rivers of Gold*, p. 137.
11. Las Casas, *A Brief Account of the Destruction of the Indies*.
12. Las Casas, *A Brief Account of the Destruction of the Indies*.

Chapter Two: Cortés's Mexican Adventure

13. Quoted in Wood, *Conquistadors*, p. 26.
14. Quoted in Patricia de Fuentes, ed., *The Conquistadors: First-Person Accounts of the Conquest of Mexico*. Norman: University of Oklahoma Press, 1993, p. 137.
15. Quoted in Fuentes, *Conquistadors: First-Person Accounts*, p. 137.
16. Anonymous, "The First Letter," in Hernán Cortés, *Letters from Mexico*, trans. and ed. Anthony Pagden. New Haven: Yale University Press, 1986, pp. 19–20. Although this letter is routinely published among Cortés's letters to the Spanish king, scholars are certain that he did not write it.
17. Wood, *Conquistadors*, p. 32.
18. Quoted in Fuentes, *Conquistadors: First-Person Accounts*, p. 138.
19. Quoted in Fuentes, *Conquistadors: First-Person Accounts*, p. 36.
20. Quoted in Miguel Leon-Portilla, ed., *The Broken Spears: The Aztec Account of the Conquest of Mexico*. Boston: Beacon, 1992, p. 51.

21. Quoted in Leon-Portilla, *The Broken Spears*, p. 23.
22. Quoted in Fuentes, *Conquistadors: First-Person Accounts*, p. 146.
23. Quoted in Fuentes, *Conquistadors: First-Person Accounts*, p. 146.

Chapter Three: The Conquest of Mexico

24. Hernán Cortés, "The Second Letter," in *Letters from Mexico*, pp. 126–27.
25. Quoted in Leon-Portilla, *The Broken Spears*, pp. 75–76.
26. Wood, *Conquistadors*, p. 72.
27. Quoted in Leon-Portilla, *The Broken Spears*, p. 77.
28. Cortés, "The Second Letter," in *Letters from Mexico*, p. 130.
29. Quoted in Fuentes, *Conquistadors: First-Person Accounts*, p. 154.
30. Quoted in Leon-Portilla, *The Broken Spears*, pp. 85–87.
31. Quoted in Leon-Portilla, *The Broken Spears*, pp. 92–93.
32. Wood, *Conquistadors*, p. 82.
33. Quoted in Leon-Portilla, *The Broken Spears*, p. 140.
34. Quoted in Fuentes, *Conquistadors: First-Person Accounts*, pp. 160–61.
35. Quoted in Fuentes, *Conquistadors: First-Person Accounts*, pp. 160–61.
36. Quoted in Leon-Portilla, *The Broken Spears*, p. 149.

Chapter Four: Spanish and Native Armies

37. Quoted in Leon-Portilla, *The Broken Spears*, p. 66.
38. Albert Marrin, *Aztecs and Spaniards: Cortes and the Conquest of Mexico.* New York: Atheneum, 1986, p. 66.
39. Marrin, *Aztecs and Spaniards*, pp. 67–68.

40. Quoted in Leon-Portilla, *The Broken Spears*, p. 30.
41. Quoted in Leon-Portilla, *The Broken Spears*, p. 30.
42. Archer Jones, *The Art of War in the Western World.* New York: Oxford University Press, 1987, p. 153.
43. Garcilaso de la Vega, *Florida of the Inca*, trans. John Varner and Jeannette Varner. Houston: University of Texas Press, 1951, p. 597.
44. Enriquez de Guzman, *The Life and Acts of Don Alonzo Enriquez de Guzman, Knight of Seville*, trans. Clements R. Markham. London: Hakluyt Society, p. 99.
45. Quoted in Fuentes, *Conquistadors: First-Person Accounts*, p. 169.
46. Quoted in Fuentes, *Conquistadors: First-Person Accounts*, p. 169.
47. Quoted in Fuentes, *Conquistadors: First-Person Accounts*, pp. 168–69.
48. Quoted in Hammond Innes, *The Conquistadors.* New York: Knopf, 1969, p. 81.

Chapter Five: Subjugation of the Incas

49. Innes, *The Conquistadors*, p. 211.
50. Wood, *Conquistadors*, p. 126.
51. Quoted in Innes, *The Conquistadors*, p. 283.
52. Quoted in John Hemming, *The Conquest of the Incas.* New York: Harcourt Brace Jovanovich, 2003, p. 39.
53. Quoted in Waman Poma, *The First New Chronicle and Good Government.* www.personal.umich.edu/~dfrye/guaman.htm.
54. Quoted in Waman Poma, *The First New Chronicle and Good Government.*

55. Quoted in Waman Poma, *The First New Chronicle and Good Government*.
56. Wood, *Conquistadors*, pp. 138–40.
57. Quoted in Hemming, *The Conquest of the Incas*, pp. 78–79.
58. Quoted in Clements R. Markham, ed. and trans., *The War of Quito and Inca Documents*. London: Hakluyt Society, p. 165.
59. Innes, *The Conquistadors*, p. 302.

Chapter Six: Voyage Down the Amazon
60. Gonzalo Fernández de Oviedo, *History of the Indies*, excerpted in Jose Toribio Medina, *The Discovery of the Amazon*, trans. H.C. Heaton. New York: AMS, 1970, pp. 391–92.
61. Gonzalo Pizarro, "Letter to the King, September 3, 1542," in Medina, *The Discovery of the Amazon*, p. 246.
62. Gaspar de Carvajal, *Discovery of the Orellana River*, in Medina, *The Discovery of the Amazon*, p. 170.
63. Carvajal, *Discovery of the Orellana River*, p. 170.
64. Pizarro, "Letter to the King," p. 250.
65. Wood, *Conquistadors*, pp. 217–18.
66. Carvajal, *Discovery of the Orellana River*, pp. 183–84.
67. Carvajal, *Discovery of the Orellana River*, p. 185.
68. Carvajal, *Discovery of the Orellana River*, pp. 190–91.
69. Carvajal, *Discovery of the Orellana River*, p. 201.

Chapter Seven: Cabeza de Vaca's Incredible Journey
70. Álvar Núñez Cabeza de Vaca, *Chronicle of the Narváez Expedition*, trans. Fanny Bandelier. New York: Penguin, 2002, p. 11.
71. Cabeza de Vaca, *Chronicle*, pp. 29–30.
72. Cabeza de Vaca, *Chronicle*, p. 30.
73. Cabeza de Vaca, *Chronicle*, p. 33.
74. Cabeza de Vaca, *Chronicle*, p. 43.
75. Cabeza de Vaca, *Chronicle*, p. 43.
76. Cabeza de Vaca, *Chronicle*, pp. 43–44.
77. Cabeza de Vaca, *Chronicle*, p. 73.
78. Cabeza de Vaca, *Chronicle*, p. 59.
79. Cabeza de Vaca, *Chronicle*, p. 93.
80. Cabeza de Vaca, *Chronicle*, p. 96.
81. Wood, *Conquistadors*, p. 262.

Epilogue: The Last Conquistador
82. Quoted in Wood, *Conquistadors*, p. 271.
83. Quoted in Stuart Stirling, *The Last Conquistador: Mansio Serra de Leguizamon and the Conquest of the Incas*. London: Sutton, 2000, pp. 141–42.

For Further Reading

Books

Hernán Cortés, *Letters from Mexico*. Trans. and ed. Anthony Pagden. New Haven: Yale University Press, 1986. The best modern translation of the letters in which Cortés described his adventures to the Spanish king.

Terrance N. D'Altroy, *The Incas*. Malden, MA: Wiley-Blackwell, 2003. A well-written examination of this important ancient people by a leading expert.

Ross Hassig, *Mexico and the Spanish Conquest*. Norman: Univerity of Oklahoma Press, 2006. Examines the military aspects of the Spanish conquest and the role played by native peoples.

John Hemming, *The Conquest of the Incas*. New York: Harcourt Brace Jovanovich, 2003. The leading modern study of the Spanish conquest of the Incas in South America.

Miguel Leon-Portilla, ed., *The Broken Spears: The Aztec Account of the Conquest of Mexico*. Boston: Beacon, 1992. An excellent translation of the riveting surviving native accounts of the Spanish conquest. Highly recommended.

John Pohl, *Aztec Warrior: A.D. 1325–1521*. Oxford, UK: Osprey, 2001. A beautifully illustrated presentation of Aztec weapons and military customs.

———, *Conquistador: 1492–1550*. Oxford, UK: Osprey, 2001. Another handsomely illustrated volume by Pohl, this one examines the conquistadors, their motives, and their weaponry.

Hugh Thomas, *Conquest: Cortes, Montezuma, and the Fall of Old Mexico*. New York: Simon & Schuster, 1995. A thorough, well-researched treatment of the subject by one of its leading experts.

———, *Rivers of Gold: The Rise of the Spanish Empire*. New York: Random House, 2005. A monumental examination of Spanish expansion in the era of Columbus and Magellan.

Richard F. Townsend, *The Aztecs*. London: Thames and Hudson, 2000. A superior, highly acclaimed study of this pivotal ancient people by a leading scholar.

Álvar Núñez Cabeza de Vaca, *Chronicle of the Narváez Expedition*. Trans. Fanny Bandelier. New York: Penguin, 2002. An easy-to-read translation of the moving first-person narrative of a shipwrecked conquistador who lived among and came to respect the Indians. Very highly recommended for readers of all ages.

Michael Wood, *Conquistadors*. Berkeley: University of California Press, 2000. A well-researched, fast-paced account of the conquistadors and their exploits. Also look for the DVD of the PBS series made in conjunction with the book.

Web Sites

The Aztecs (http://library.thinkquest. org/16325/y-main.html). A good general reference on the ancient Aztecs with several links to articles about various aspects of their culture.

The Conquistadors (www.pbs.org/con quistadors/index.html). Home page of the informative PBS documentary on the subject, based on the book by Michael Wood.

Eyewitnesses to the Conquistadors (www.pbs.org/conquistadors/index. html). Easy-to-read translations of three original accounts of the Spanish conquests in the Americas, including one of Cortés's letters.

The Inca (www.mnsu.edu/emuseum/ prehistory/latinamerica/south/cul tures/inca.html). An excellent brief overview of Inca civilization.

The Myth of Quetzalcoatl (www. rjames.com/Toltec/myth2.htm). An information-packed synopsis of the native story of a past leader whom the Aztecs initially identified with the Spaniard Cortés.

The Spanish Empire (http://encarta. msn.com/encyclopedia_761595536/ spanish_empire.html). An excellent general overview of the rise of Spain's empire.

Index

atlatl, 49–50, *50*
cannons, 45–48, *48*
firearms, 47–48
of natives, 49–52, 54
Spanish, 27, 45–48
steel, 46–47

Wood, Michael
    on Amazon River, 73
    on Cabeza de Vaca, 87
    on conquistadors, 8
    on Pizarros, 59
    on Spanish weapons, 27

Picture Credits

In addition to his acclaimed volumes on the ancient world, historian Don Nardo has written and edited many books for young adults about medieval history (including *The Inquisition, The Black Death,* and *The Trial of Galileo*) and modern history (including *The French Revolution, The Salem Witch Trials, The Mexican-American War, The Great Depression,* and *World War II in the Pacific*). Nardo also writes screenplays and teleplays and composes music. He lives with his wife Christine in Massachusetts.